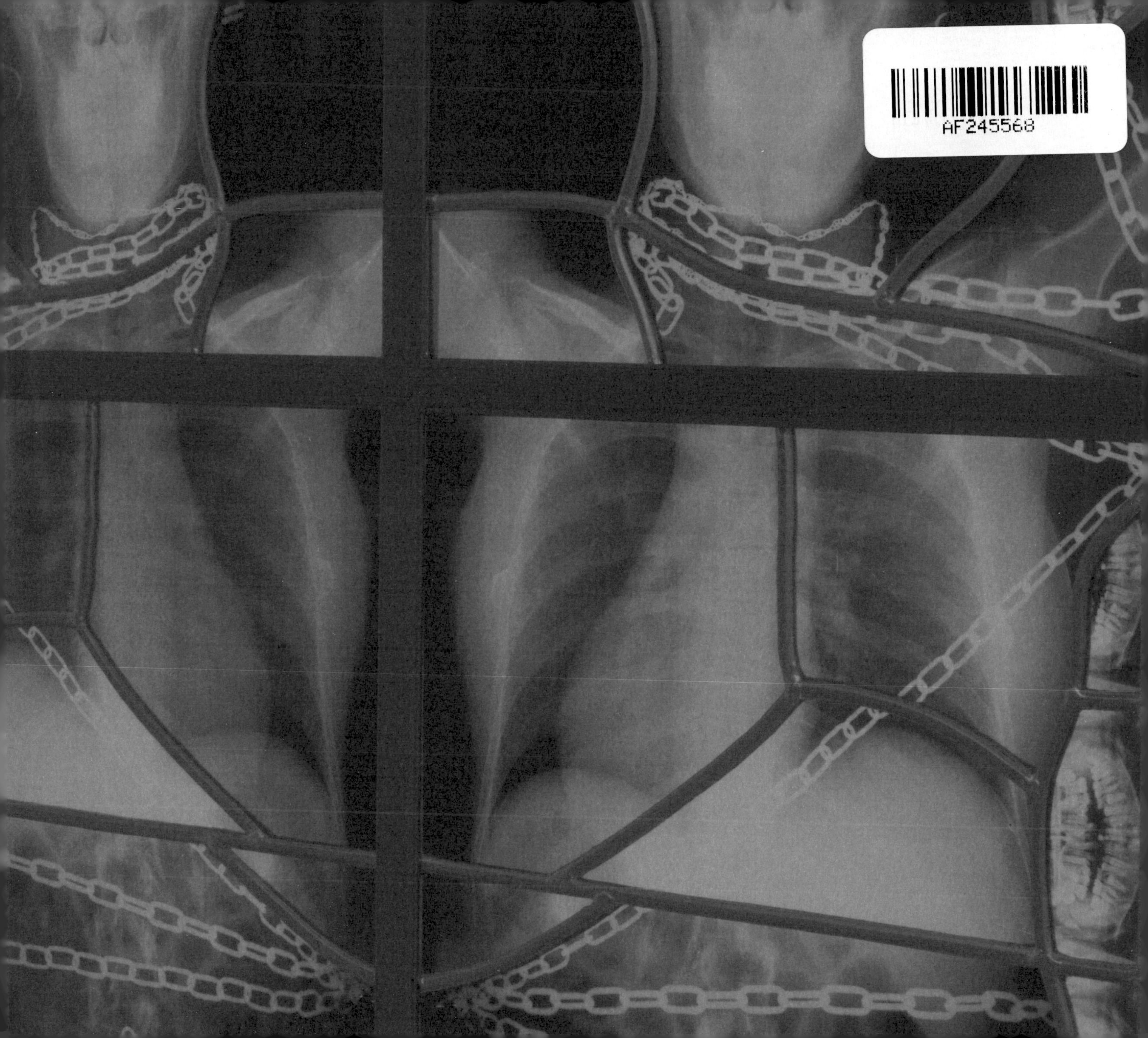
AF245568

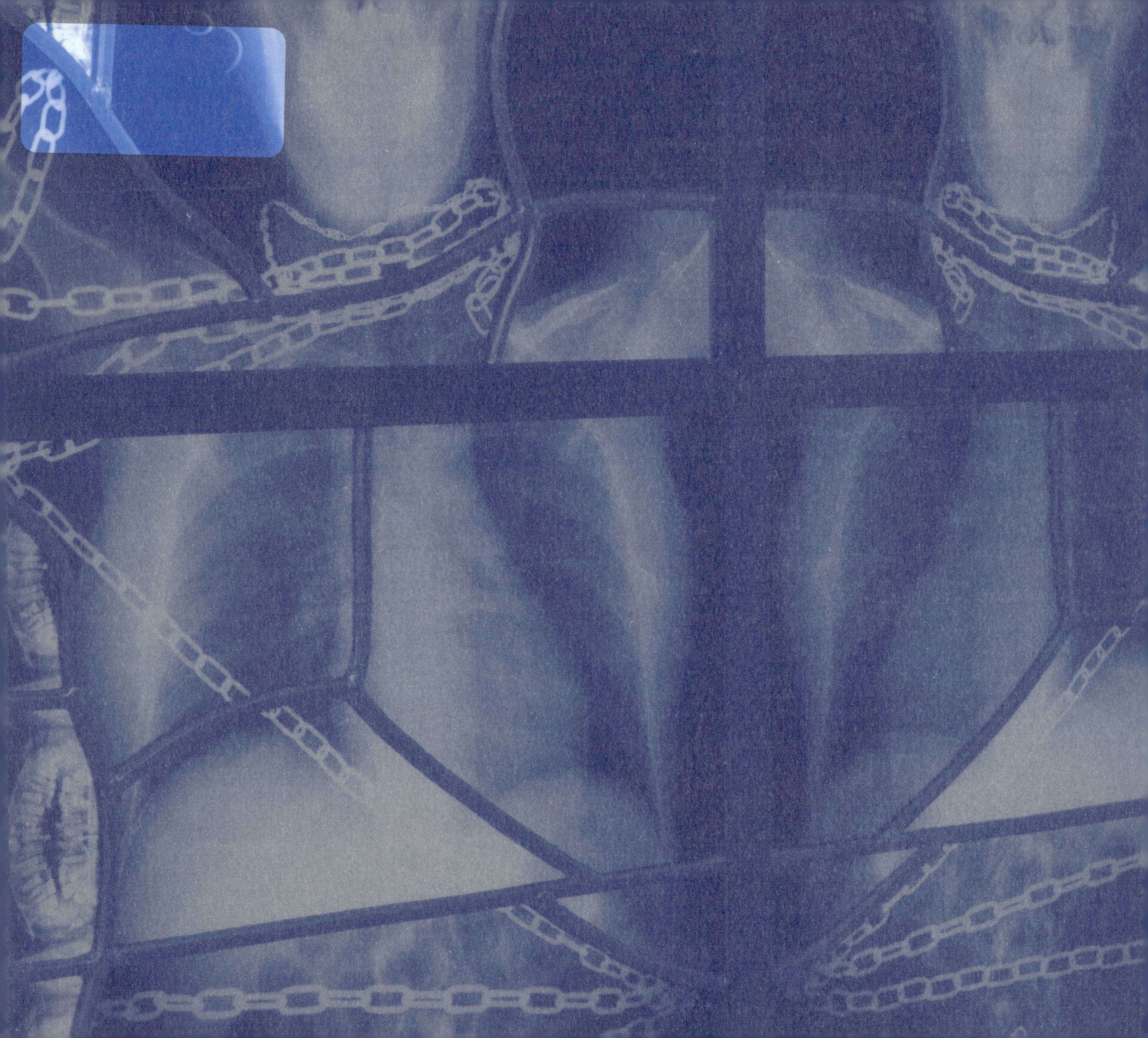

MINING GLASS

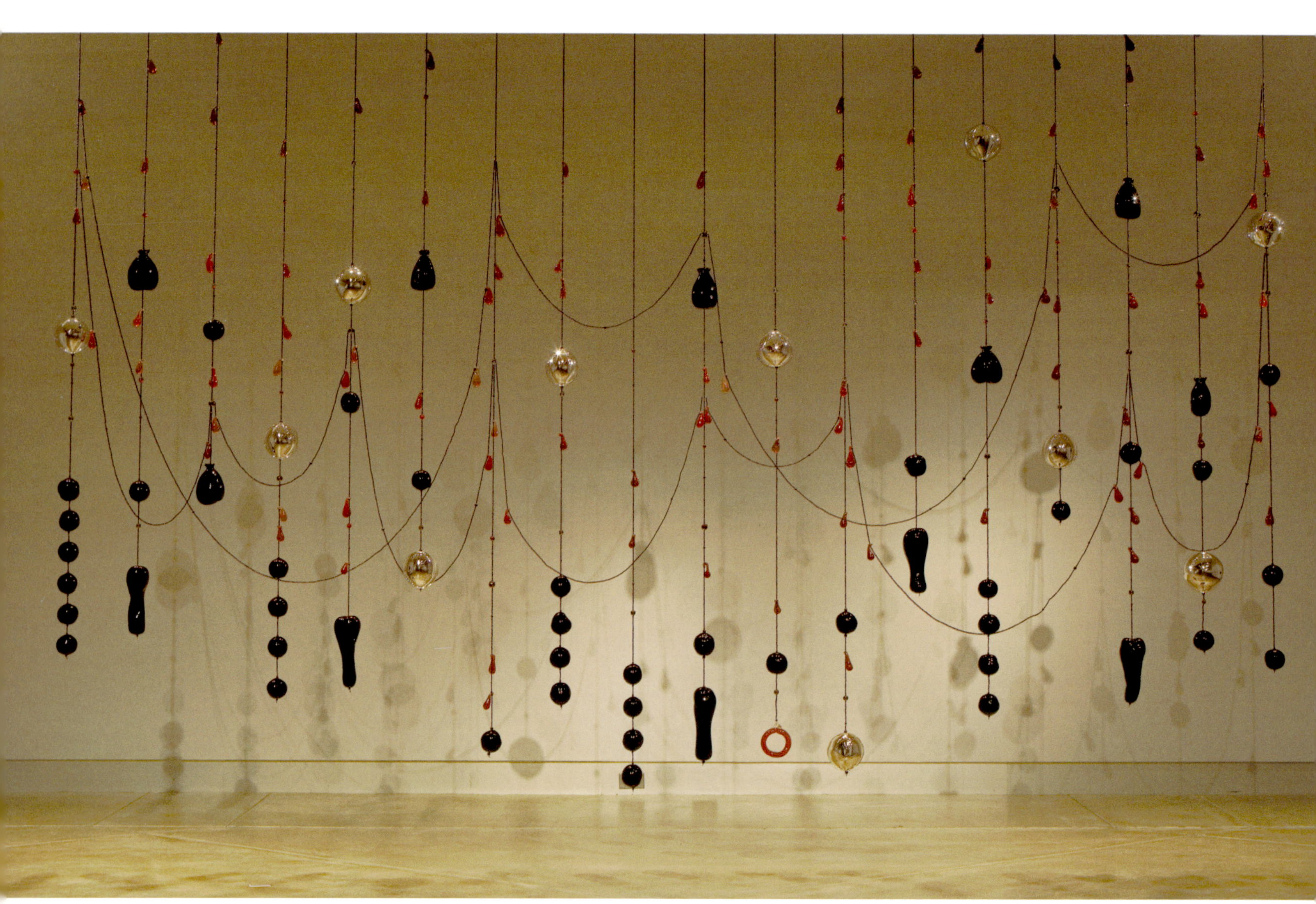

by Juli Cho Bailer

MINING GLASS

Wim Delvoye
Teresita Fernández
Mona Hatoum
Maya Lin
Jean-Michel Othoniel
Kiki Smith
Fred Wilson
Chen Zhen

MUSEUM OF GLASS

TACOMA, WASHINGTON

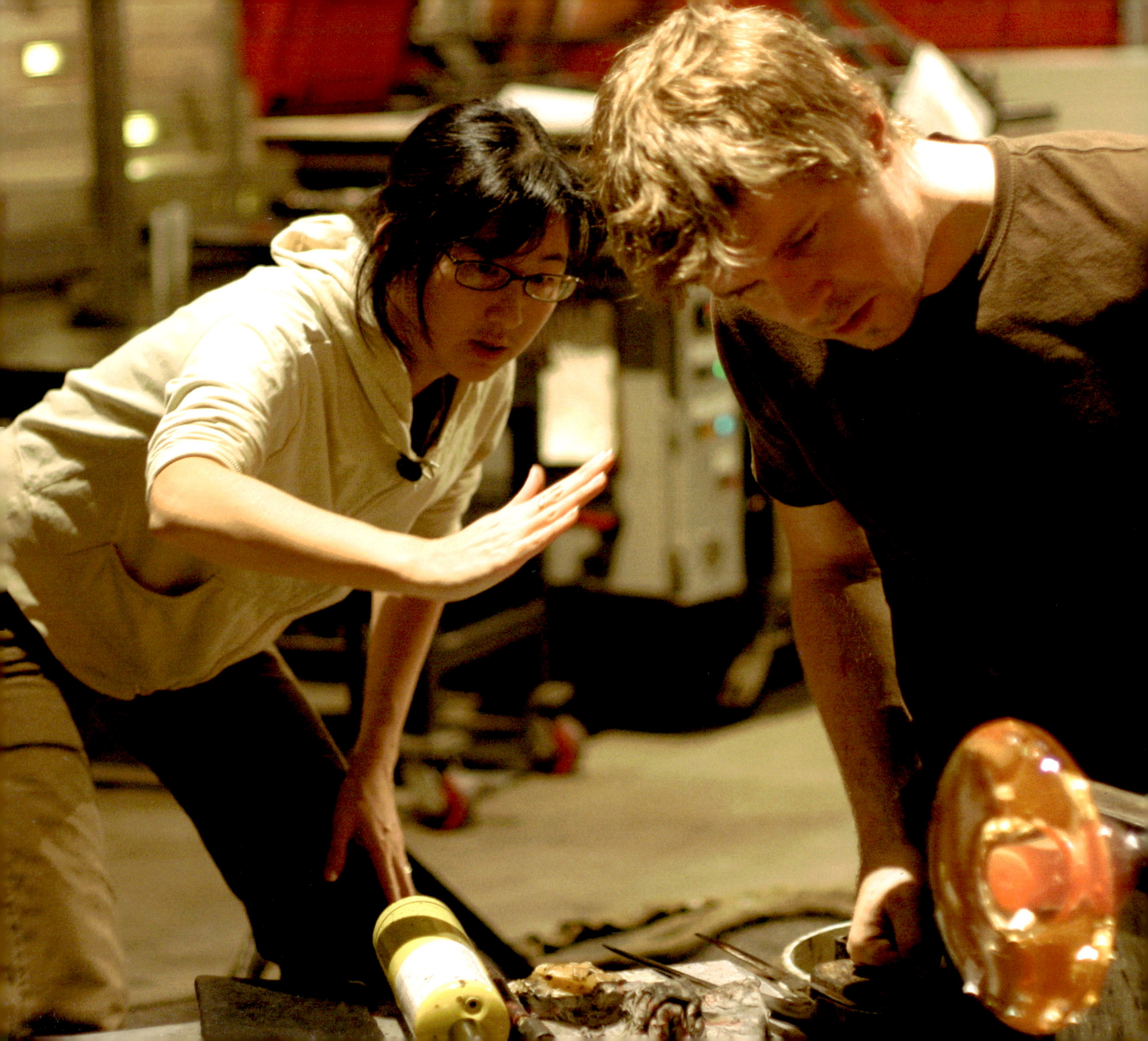

Timothy Close

Director/CEO

The Museum of Glass is proud to celebrate our Fifth Anniversary with this unparalleled exhibition featuring eight internationally established and influential artists who have applied glass in their astonishingly diverse oeuvres. Presenting important installations created since 2000, the artists in *Mining Glass*—Wim Delvoye, Teresita Fernández, Mona Hatoum, Maya Lin, Jean-Michel Othoniel, Kiki Smith, Fred Wilson, and the late Chen Zhen—demonstrate how the distinctive qualities of this medium are increasingly being drawn upon in contemporary artistic practice.

We extend our heartfelt thanks to the extraordinary artists whose works are presented in this exhibition and documented in this publication. We are exceptionally grateful to Maya Lin and Jean-Michel Othoniel for their commitment to this project and for taking time out of their busy schedules to conceive stunning new installations—and to create them in the Museum's Hot Shop Amphitheater. This unique experience gave our visitors an exclusive opportunity to witness the creative process of these remarkable talents. We are also honored to present Fred Wilson in the Hot Shop in August this year and thank him for allowing us to add him to the list of distinguished Visiting Artist residents.

We could not have realized this exhibition and catalogue without the steadfast support and assistance of the artists' representatives and studios: Douglas Baxter, PaceWildenstein; Alexandra Bradley, White Cube; Xu-Min Chen, widow of Chen Zhen; Katie Commodore, Maya Lin Studio; Gianni Degryse, Wim Delvoye Studio; Justin Eagle, White Cube; Jan Endlich, Lehmann Maupin; Alice Fontanelli, Galleria Continua; Raphaël Gatel, Galerie Emmanuel Perrotin; Sophie Greig, White Cube; Ellen Holdorf, PaceWildenstein; Elizabeth Littlejohn, formerly of Lehmann Maupin; Olivier Lounissi, Jean-Michel Othoniel Studio; Charlie Manzo, PaceWildenstein; Gabriela Mizes, Podesta Collection; Kristina Schonberg, Lehmann Maupin; and the Gagosian Gallery. In addition to the artists and galleries who generously agreed to lend the works, we are truly grateful to Heather and Anthony Podesta for allowing us to include an important work from their collection.

Mining Glass was artfully conceived by Juli Cho Bailer, exhibition curator. Numerous staff lent invaluable expertise and assistance to Ms. Cho Bailer in realizing and organizing this exhibition and catalogue: Rosanna Sharpe, former director of curatorial affairs; Oscar Tuazon, exhibition designer; Rebecca Engelhardt, registrar and collections manager; Tyson Griffin, curatorial assistant; Liz Cepanec, visiting artist program manager; and William Bitter, preparator. We also thank Michelle Dunn Marsh of Dunn Design, who is responsible for the publication's elegant presentation, and Sigrid Asmus for her detailed editorial review.

Finally, with great appreciation, we wish to acknowledge The Paul G. Allen Family Foundation, Museum of Glass Board of Trustees, Russell Investment Group, the National Endowment for the Arts, Click! Network, the Art Alliance for Contemporary Glass, and Selden's Home Furnishings for their commitment and support of this exhibition.

Maya Lin directing the fabrication of a glass element for the installation *Dew Point*, with gaffer Janusz Pozniak at the bench. Lin's Visiting Artist Residency took place at the Museum of Glass on March 16 and 17, 2007. Photo courtesy of Museum of Glass.

Juli Cho Bailer

Mining Glass brings together eight internationally established artists—Wim Delvoye (Belgium), Teresita Fernández (United States), Mona Hatoum (Great Britain), Maya Lin (United States), Jean-Michel Othoniel (France), Kiki Smith (United States), Fred Wilson (United States), and the late Chen Zhen (China)—whose prominent use of glass invites a closer examination into the way this protean medium has expanded beyond its traditional application in decorative and functional art.

At this moment, many artists are at work *mining* glass for its unparalleled multiplicity of form as well as its rich and complex associations. The sheer abundance of striking works made in glass allows us to reflect upon some of the fundamental issues with which artists grapple today. Their work offers a new and deeper understanding and appreciation of glass, not only as a medium in its own right, but also in the ways artists are approaching it. This forthright use of the medium has not always been the case. With very few exceptions, glass as a sculptural material is effectively absent from the canon of modern art. In the early twentieth century, in *The Bride Stripped Bare by Her Bachelors, Even* (1915–23), also known as *The Large Glass*, Marcel Duchamp made use of the apparent insubstantiality and diaphanous qualities of glass for his meticulous oil-paint, lead wire, and lead foil composition. At once an architectural, window-like component that would further enhance his technical rendering, the sheets of glass also functioned to obscure the

brushwork or painterly effects, thereby removing the hand of the artist. By contrast, while Duchamp was preoccupied with his theoretical writings, his readymades, and his unconventional approach to painting, which together ambitiously challenged basic definitions of art and taste, the decorative arts were experiencing a cross-disciplinary artistic spirit of their own, as artists such as Émile Gallé, Louis Comfort Tiffany, and René Lalique, who had been formally trained as painters, undertook their glass creations in the elegant and refined styles of Art Nouveau and Art Deco.

Even as the twentieth century saw a major expansion in the media employed in sculpture, glass seldom made an appearance. However, in the 1960s Larry Bell, working within the reductivist principles set forth by Minimalism, began constructing geometric cubes of metal-plated and etched-glass panes, while Christopher Wilmarth incorporated frosted-glass sheets into his architectonic steel sculptures to optically lighten the geometric rigor of intersecting lines and planes. In the late 1960s, a group of artists began to move away from the rigidity and severity of Minimalism to develop a new sculptural expression, Postminimalism, also known as "process art" because it was concerned with the specific processes of making and perceiving the work as much as with its structure and finish. These artists turned to nontraditional materials, such as plastics, neon, sand, salt, felt, rubber, fiberglass, and glass, and began to abandon mass and verticality—some of sculpture's key attributes—in favor of less-organized, haphazard arrangements that placed an emphasis on horizontality. The hand of the artist became intentionally apparent again—often with stretching and

"It's useful to think that you choose materials just the way you'd choose words." —Kiki Smith

modeling, but also in the seemingly random acts of throwing, pouring, and scattering—and introduced a new kind of gesture into sculpture. Yet the gestural impulse evident in the works of artists such as Robert Smithson, Richard Serra, Barry Le Va, and Eva Hesse was chiefly deployed in the use of common industrial materials. Glass, when it was used, continued even then to be commercial plate or mirrored glass—and it was expressly void of ornamentation. Studio or sculpted glass in the decorative arts tradition was as yet not considered to have a place in advanced sculpture.

The 1960s and 1970s also saw the emergence of feminist art, as well as the craft, studio glass, and pattern and decoration movements. These movements brought forward artists who had begun with traditional training in wood, clay, textiles, metals, and glass, but who had elevated their work to such a high aesthetic level that labeling it as functional or decorative was no longer appropriate. This fresh creative spirit invited other artists to consciously draw inspiration from the artisanal traditions operating outside the mainstream of sanctioned art. Practices once denigrated as craft, unsophisticated, or associated with women and non-Western people—weaving, knitting, sewing, quilting, embroidering, pottery, and glassblowing—opened new avenues for these artists, who were now poised to openly challenge the stigma that modern art had placed on anything remotely resembling ornamentation and functionality. Ultimately, artists validated craft and decorative arts techniques by appropriating them to meet conceptual objectives.

In the 1980s, Postmodernism, with its promotion of multiculturalism and its hybridization practices, paved the way for a truly multifarious approach to making art, one that continues to permeate the current artistic climate. Today, the blurring of boundaries is an obvious and crucial aspect of our wider culture—creatively combining architecture, performance, fashion, furniture design, and even lifestyle culture. The fact that manufactured and handmade, precious and mundane, or severe and assertively flamboyant objects can all participate in the same artistic discourse is emblematic of the contemporary experience. The new millennium also brought further changes to bear in attitudes toward beauty in art. Beauty, previously shunned as if it were an inconsequential feature, has been reestablished as a legitimate component of art, allowing us to consider glass—perhaps one of the most seductive and beautiful of materials—with unabashed admiration.

Fine objects, celebrated purely for their splendor and excellence, are nevertheless out of place in the context of contemporary art practices. Going against that grain, the artists brought together here demonstrate the ease

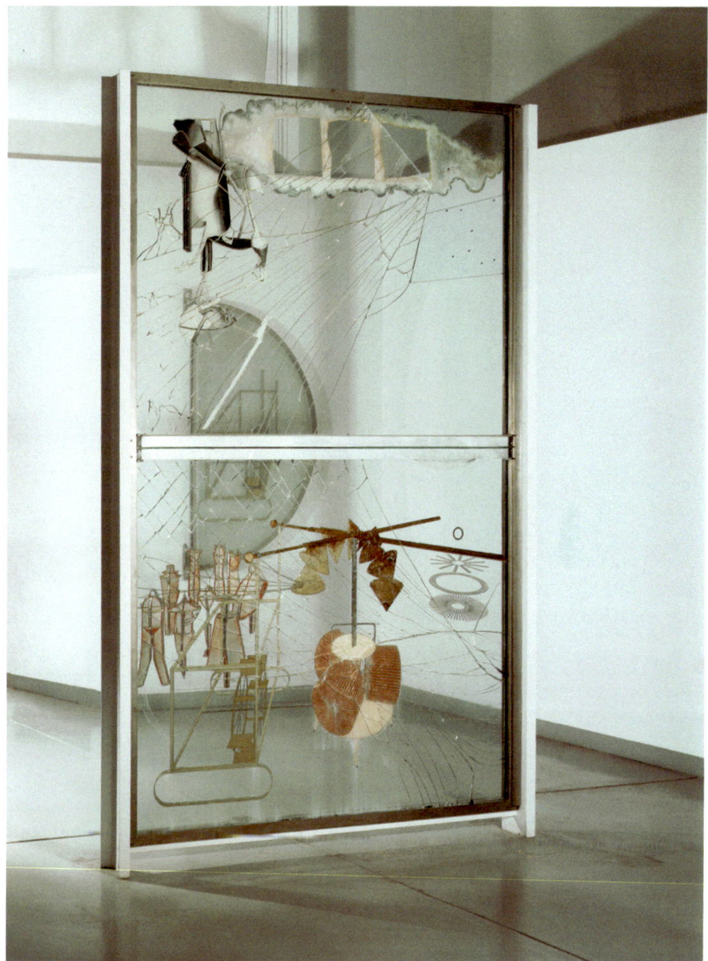

Marcel Duchamp (American, born France 1887; died 1968). *The Bride Stripped Bare by Her Bachelors, Even (The Large Glass)*, 1915–23; Oil, varnish, lead foil, lead wire, and dust on two glass panels. 109 ¼ x 69 ¼ (277 x 175 cm). Bequest of Katherine S. Dreier, 1952, Collection of Philadelphia Museum of Art. © Artists Rights Society (ARS), New York / ADAGP, Paris / Estate of Marcel Duchamp

with which they move from material to material, from form to form, as well as a shared tendency toward the experiential element of art. This quality is evidenced by a number of factors, including their preference for installation—characteristically established by the elimination of the pedestal as conventionalized by Minimalism, the removal of a viewing frame in favor of near or complete immersion in the artwork, and reliance on seriality or similarity or multiple forms (to which blowing and casting glass lends itself

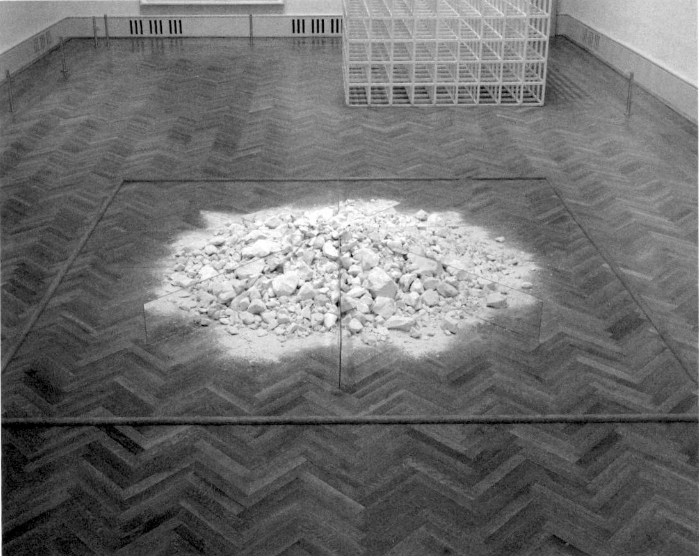

Robert Smithson (American, 1938–1973); *Chalk-Mirror Displacement*, 1969. Sixteen mirrors (eight one-sided mirrors placed back to back to form eight sections) and chalk. 10 feet diameter (305 cm). Through prior gift of Mr. and Mrs. Edward Morris, 1987.277, collection of The Art Institute of Chicago © Estate of Robert Smithson / Licensed by VAGA, New York City, photo courtesy of The Art Institute of Chicago

well). All of these devices help to further destabilize the notion that a work of art must be single, unique, and made by the artist's hands—and therefore dearly cherished on a single pedestal.

The artists in *Mining Glass*—coming from cultural backgrounds as diverse as the United States, Latin America, Europe, the Middle East, and Asia, as well as from assorted disciplines in painting, sculpture, architecture, public art, curating, theater, and performance art—began their careers heavily influenced by the last few decades of revisionist art criticism and practice. It

is thus important to understand that their works are not primarily aimed at the legitimization of craft or the decorative arts, nor with the validation of any one particular material or technique. Rather, their production embraces a stunning diversity of materials and approaches that are unified in an open-ended manner that allows viewers to become authors of their own meanings.

Some of these artists, no doubt, have benefited from the advancements of American Studio Glass. The increased accessibility of working in glass today is generally credited to the achievements of that movement, and the subsequent propagation of hot shops, MFA programs in glassblowing, and glass art residencies all over the world, which offer to both novice and expert the means and instruction necessary to surmount the tremendous learning curve required to work molten hot glass into sculptural form—one does not simply pick up a glassblower's pipe one day as one might a stick of graphite.

Glass has an exceptional and rich tradition that begins very early in human history, and goes well beyond twentieth-century art-historical movements. Obsidian, a natural volcanic glass, has been used since the Stone Age, when it was worked to form arrows and blades that not only served a practical function but were also used in rituals, such as bloodletting and scarification ceremonies; it was also carved into jewelry, amulets, and effigies. Moreover, primitive cultures polished obsidian into mirrors that were thought to have magical powers, objects that were believed to function as a threshold between the earthly and divine worlds.

The transmutable character of glass has fascinated people for centuries, and manipulating or transforming the substance—through the use of fire—was once even viewed as a sort of wizardry. In this sense, we can consider how the production of glass might have been compared to alchemy, accounting perhaps for its recurring appearance in fairy stories. Glass—as in the glass slippers worn by Cinderella, or the glass coffin that preserved Snow White—can be interpreted symbolically as a magical medium that assists the transformation from girl to woman. (Charles Perrault substituted glass for gold in his seventeenth-century version of Cinderella, which tells something about the value of glass in that period). Even in a fairy tale, one would guess glass shoes would be difficult to dance in, thus the tale's trust in the delicate but also enchanting quality of glass—with its smooth visual translation into ice, snow, diamonds, or wax. Perrault describes the charmed moment when Cinderella tries on the glass slipper and how the Prince "saw it slipped on as easily, and fitted as perfectly, as if it were made of wax."[1] Bronze and iron can also be melted and reshaped in comparable ways, yet as handsome as bronze is, neither it nor iron can elicit the same emotional response as glass.

The duality of glass—precious, magical, and mystical, yet common, practical, and functional—certainly lends it a textural richness, making it an attractive choice for contemporary artists who are more scrupulous than

ever about the connotations of the myriad materials available to them. By contrast, the artistry of glass in earlier centuries stressed technical mastery of the medium by the artisan, a convention that still influences much of glass art-making today. It is this aspect of the artisan's mastery that may conceivably be seen as a challenge when considering the works in *Mining Glass*, since all of the glass elements were conceived by the artists, yet fabricated by others. However, this fact only emphasizes how far glass has moved beyond its restricted use as a decorative medium used exclusively in the traditional circles of glass masters. Work in glass, like that in other materials, has now joined the broader mainstream of art, where it is not unusual for the actual fabrication of art objects to be undertaken by others, albeit under strict supervision of the artist. This advance also means that the works brought together for this exhibition, created using a variety of long-established techniques, are—first and foremost—conceptually developed.

---

1. *The Complete Fairy Tales of Charles Perrault*, translated by Neil Philip and Nicoletta Simboroski. (New York: Clarion Books, 1993), p. 68.

All that is true, yet artists nonetheless often find their conceptual inspiration in a particular material, as does Fred Wilson, who arrived at fabricating sculpture in blown glass after two decades of rigorous investigatory installations that recontextualized existing cultural material; and Jean-Michel Othoniel, who first became obsessed with glass through his research on obsidian, which has since led to the exclusive use of glass in his extravagant sculpture. For Maya Lin, glass seems the perfect conduit to channel the artist's personal meditations on the purity of landscape, while Teresita Fernández includes shimmering glass beads among a host of favored synthetic materials that make up her reconstructions of natural phenomena. Mona Hatoum's many travels and residencies frequently determine her choice of material, and more instinctively than deliberately, Hatoum has repeatedly turned to glass—from flameworked laboratory test-tubes, to bottle glass produced by a factory in Thiers, France, to handblown lead-crystal spheres fabricated in Colle di Val d'Elsa, Italy, world renowned for its crystal. Similarly, one of Wim Delvoye's artistic strategies is to work with artisanal traditions, such as the stained-glass techniques devoted to adorning Gothic cathedrals, to suit his own artistic agenda. Many of the artists, but most prominently Kiki Smith, Mona Hatoum, and the late Chen Zhen, fold an inexhaustible range of materials and objects into their visual vocabularies—from ordinary found objects to exquisitely fabricated pieces in bronze, marble, alabaster, porcelain, and, of course, glass.

As they do with any medium they work with, these artists integrate glass into their respective existing lexicons without contriving a message to make it fit. Clearly and intentionally selected for its extraordinary potential and complex cultural and metaphorical allusions, glass assumes a variety of appearances, from the minimal to the rococo. The material we see in *Mining Glass* is delicate, opulent, shimmering, luminous, spectral, evocative, poignant, and unforgettable, and we can follow these qualities on the narrative journeys offered throughout the exhibition—excess, artifice, boundaries, landscape, desire, enchantment, identity, and intersections. Together, these suggest passages through which we can see beyond the technical matters that overwhelm our appreciation of glass and begin to observe and understand the deeper issues that concern artists today.

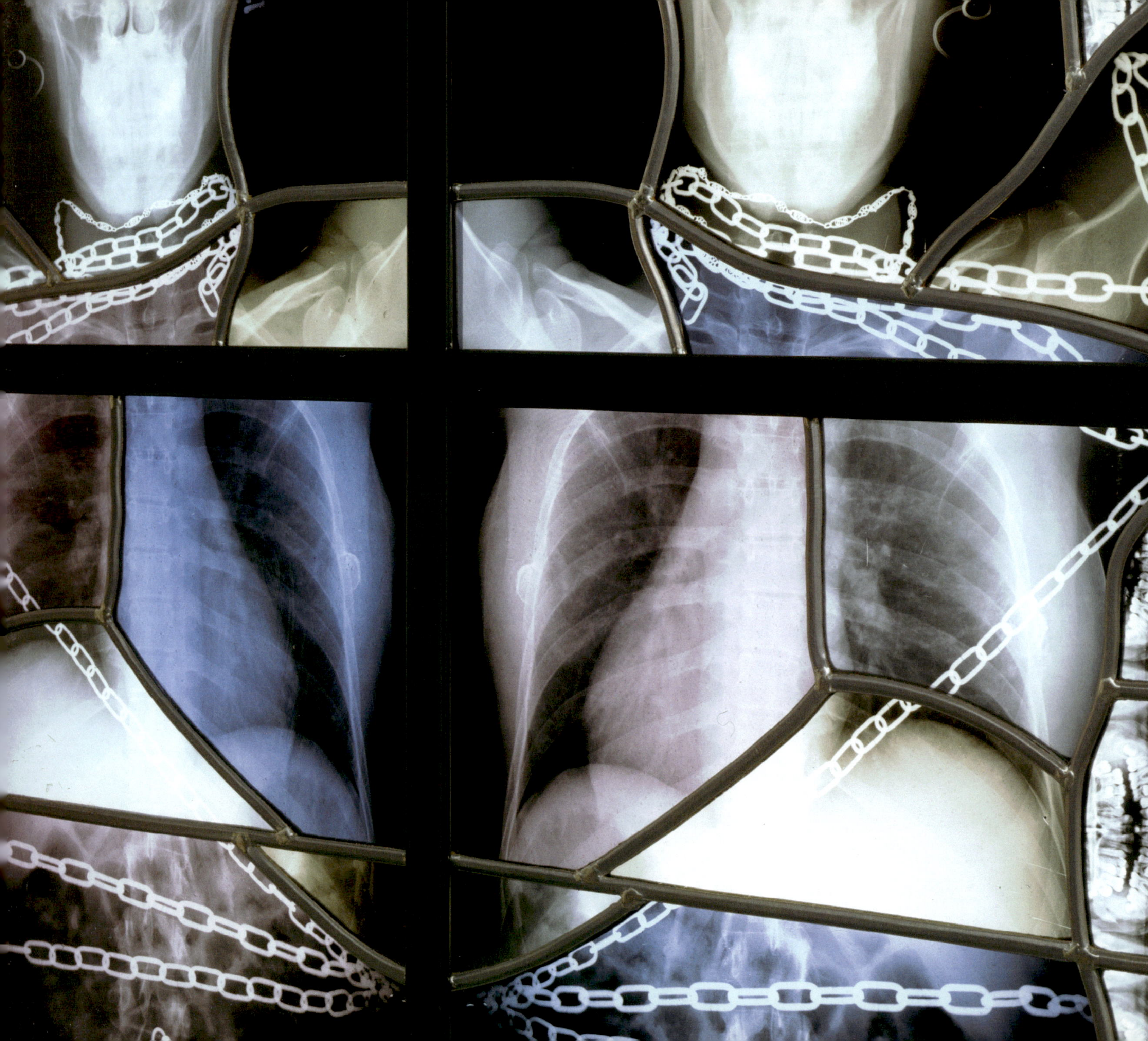

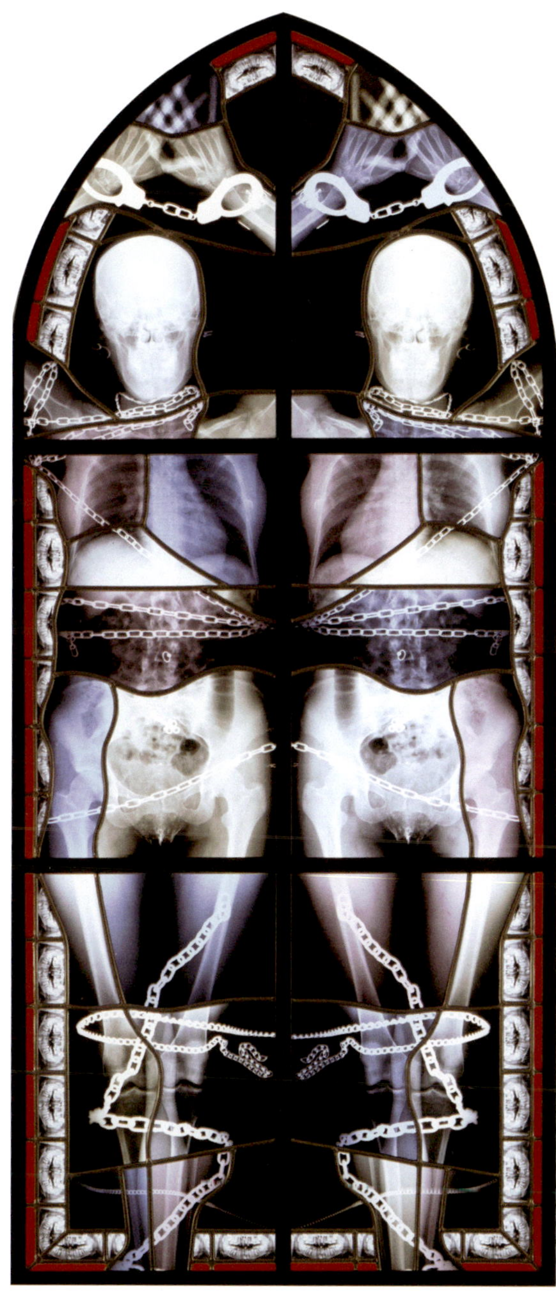

Wim Delvoye

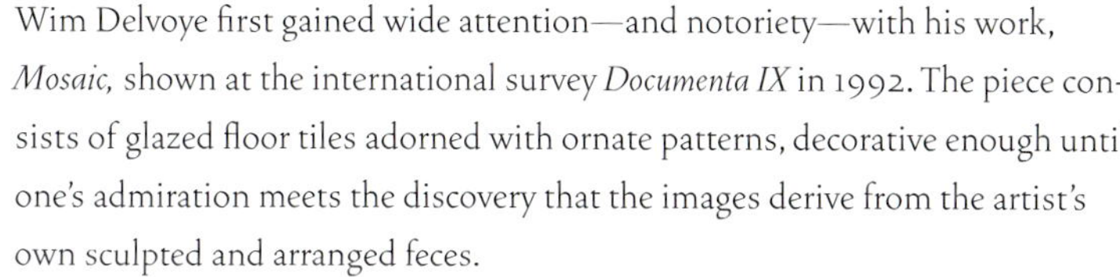

Wim Delvoye first gained wide attention—and notoriety—with his work, *Mosaic,* shown at the international survey *Documenta IX* in 1992. The piece consists of glazed floor tiles adorned with ornate patterns, decorative enough until one's admiration meets the discovery that the images derive from the artist's own sculpted and arranged feces.

Much of Delvoye's art relies on a strategy of provocatively juxtaposing opposites—high and low culture, fine arts and craft, celestial ideas and agrarian traditions, transcendental aspirations and crude bodily functions—to expose the irony and paradox of our art-historical legacy and culture. Delvoye's 2001 series, *Nine Muses,* includes nine backlit, stained-glass windows, each named after one of the classic arts, and features X-ray, sonogram, and MRI composites of copulating and cavorting couples alongside gothic skeletal outlines and tangled intestinal images. The optical trickery employed in his tiled floor series is also evident as Delvoye appropriates the rich historical tradition of illuminating cathedral space through windows illustrating sacred imagery while presenting scientifically produced, explicit imagery.

To stage his complex investigations of the abject, Delvoye borrows heavily from deep artisanal traditions of ornamentation and decoration. His work both challenges the value of the high arts and subverts accepted notions of decorum and social conventions about sex and nudity, and in doing so questions our relationship to consumer society and the culture of excess.

Left and above: *Calliope* from Nine Muses Series, 2001–2002

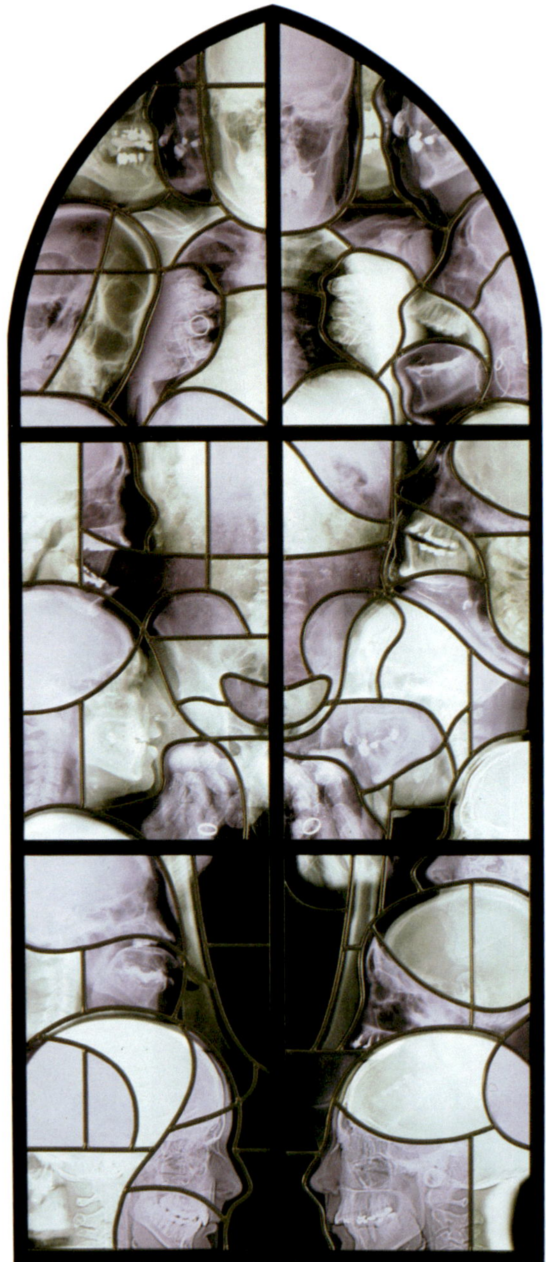

  Melpomene from Nine Muses Series, 2001–2002

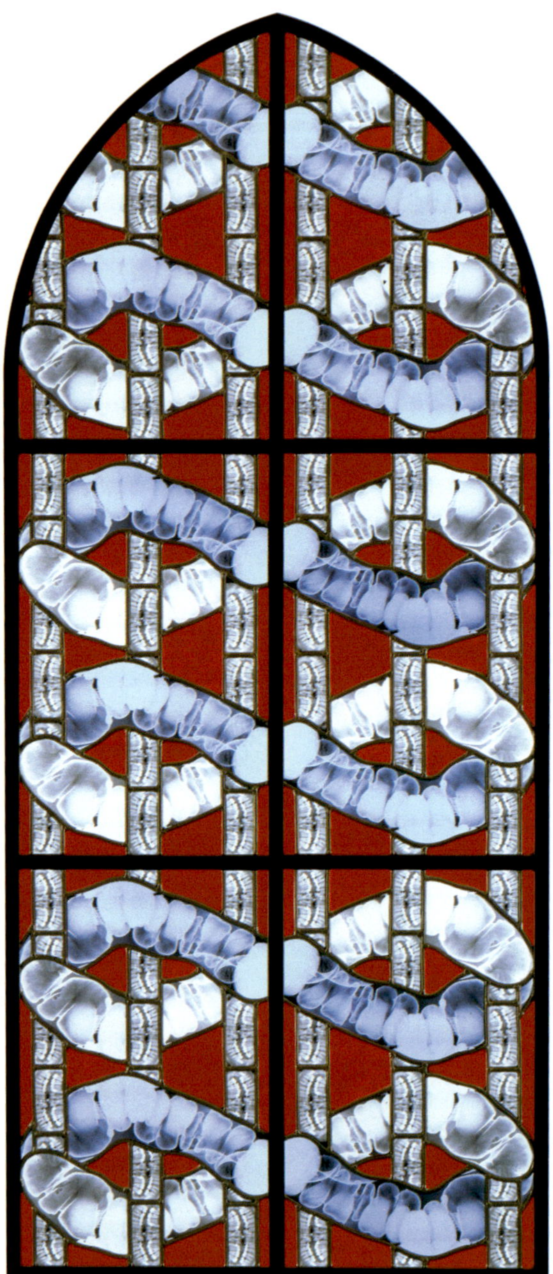

Terpsichore from Nine Muses Series, 2001–2002

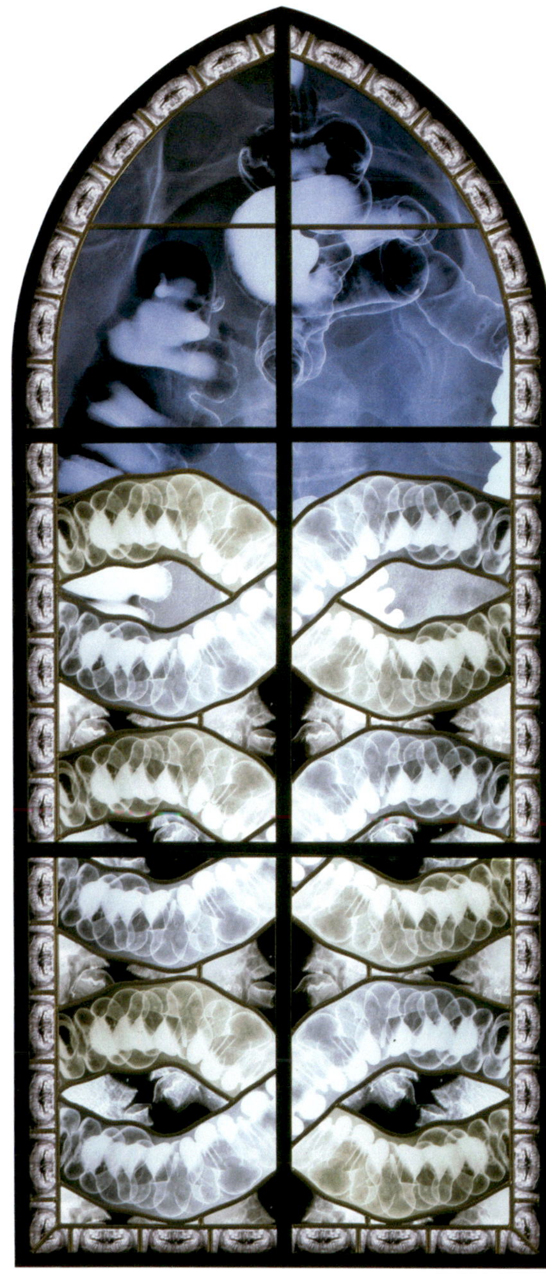

Clio from Nine Muses Series, 2001–2002

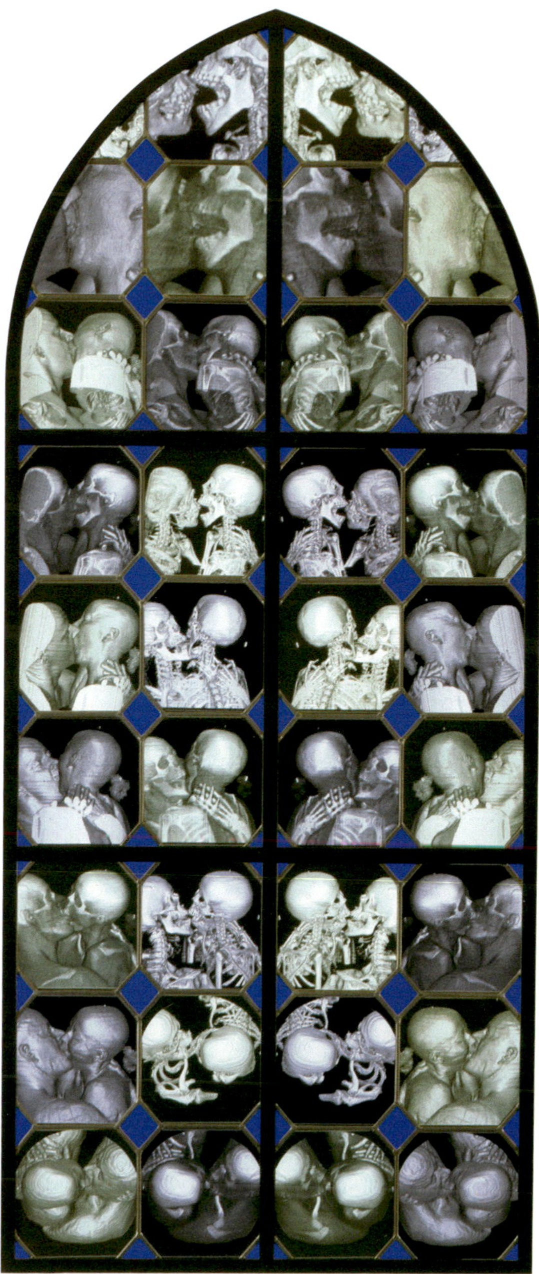

Erato from Nine Muses Series, 2001–2002

Teresita Fernández

Teresita Fernández invites us to look at the natural world through her carefully conceived and elegantly polished works that offer a sensorial experience of nature and its phenomena. Like many artists of her generation, she draws us into a discourse on the relationship between the organic and the artificial through an exceptionally subtle and intelligent investigation that also examines our invention of and intervention in landscape, as it is reflected in her pared-down and refined approach to reconstructing undulating sand dunes, cascading waterfalls, billowing clouds, and blazing fires. Fernández favors industrial and synthetic materials. Simple plastic, vinyl, acrylic, aluminum, and glass are coupled with the clever yet unfussy perceptual strategies that she uses to maximum effect. Her minimal sculptures and architectural constructions evoke the essence of marvels found in nature, from desert landscapes to botanical gardens.

In *Eruption (Large)* of 2005, thousands of tiny, shimmering glass beads are strewn over a vinyl and aluminum palette resembling, in its curvaceous form and radiant color, a pool of lava. The ancient Egyptians believed glass beads held charmed powers and there is something suggestive of this heightened feeling in Fernández's visually magical invention that hovers gracefully and buoyantly above the ground.

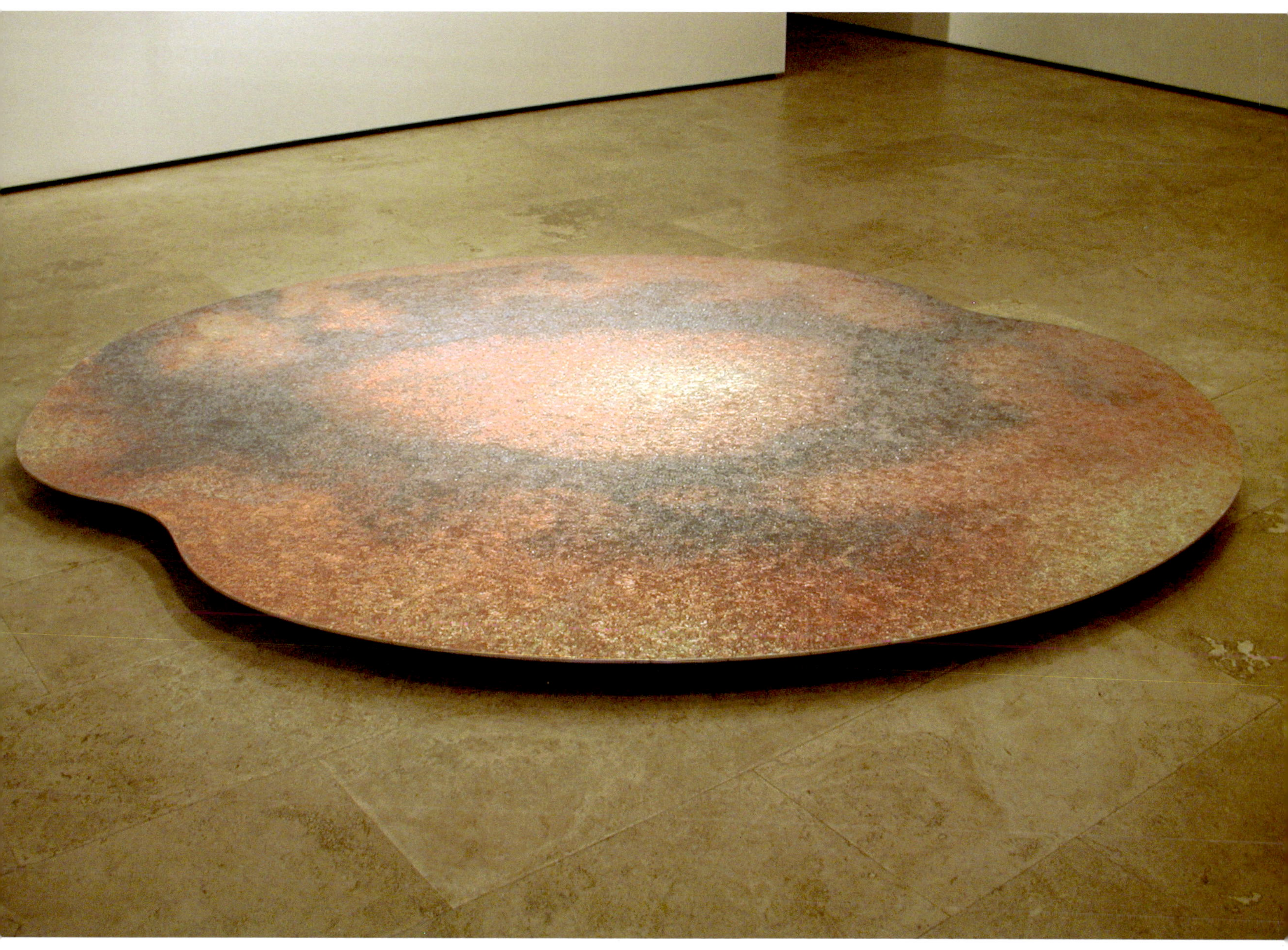

Eruption (Large), 2005

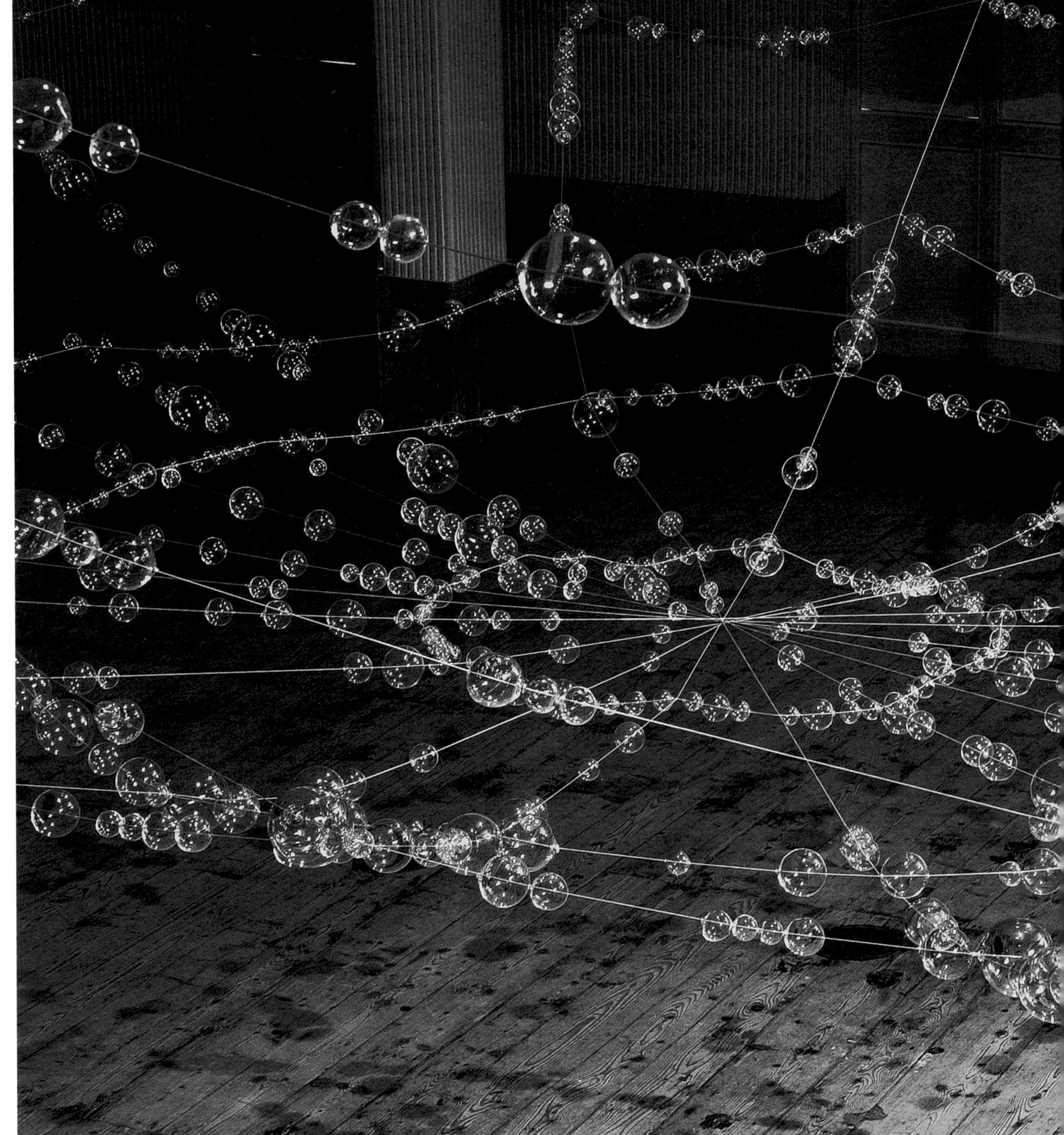

Mona Hatoum

Mona Hatoum's earlier works, particularly her confrontational performances, analyze institutional power structures as they impinge on issues of identity important to her as a woman, as a person of non-Western origin, and her extraordinary circumstances as a person in exile. In the early 1990s, however, Hatoum moved that more private meditation toward universal themes in a visually and psychologically arresting language that addresses issues of the home and the homeland, unrest, security, and boundaries, as delineated by geography as well as by society.

Hatoum often alludes to the body in her work, both directly, as in the use of her own hair, and subtly, as through the references to its life made implicitly by household objects. Domestic routines such as weaving (with hair), knitting (with pasta), and cooking (with kitchen tools) are closely joined with her interest in objects associated with imprisonment—cages, lockers, prisoners' beds, and webs—reminding us of captivity and our restricted movement in the homeland as well as in the home.

Hatoum's immense *Web* (2006) uses the graphic lines found in many of her installations, but this time places the viewer's own body just below a network of wires. Far from being a sinewy, organic creation, Hatoum's spare representation involves stainless steel and glass spheres—each globe perfectly transparent and contained—suggesting that if the tidy cells perhaps represent our attempt to control our chaotic lives, they are as see-through and breakable as glass.

Web, 2006

Maya Lin

In addition to Maya Lin's renowned public monuments, such as the Vietnam
Veterans Memorial, whose design catapulted her to fame while she was still
a student at Yale, her highly refined art encompasses architecture, furniture
design, studio works, and immensely scaled land-art installations—most recently her *Confluence Project*, a series of installations along the Columbia River
commissioned to commemorate the Lewis and Clark Expedition of 1804–06.

A deep respect for the earth resounds throughout Lin's pure forms that
owe their intensity to the meticulous analytic research that she often seeks
out as she conceives her work. In her career of more than twenty years, Lin's
sensitivity for the organic has grown in power and sensitivity, taking shape
in introspective, subtle, and fluid works that integrate themselves harmoni-
ously into their environments and invite us to take a closer look at the world
around us. Using mostly natural or recyclable materials—stone, wood, water,
glass—but also topographical technologies, Lin responds to the inherent character of each to reinterpret landscapes, geological formations, and phenomena
found in nature, from avalanches and groundswells to the undulating depths
of the ocean floor.

For *Dew Point* (2007), Lin worked together with the Hot Shop team at the
Museum of Glass during her residency, where she created this installation of
hot-sculpted clear glass forms. The shapes suggest water drops, and evoke the
tranquility of a Zen garden, yet also clearly remind us of the alarming depletion
of this essential resource.

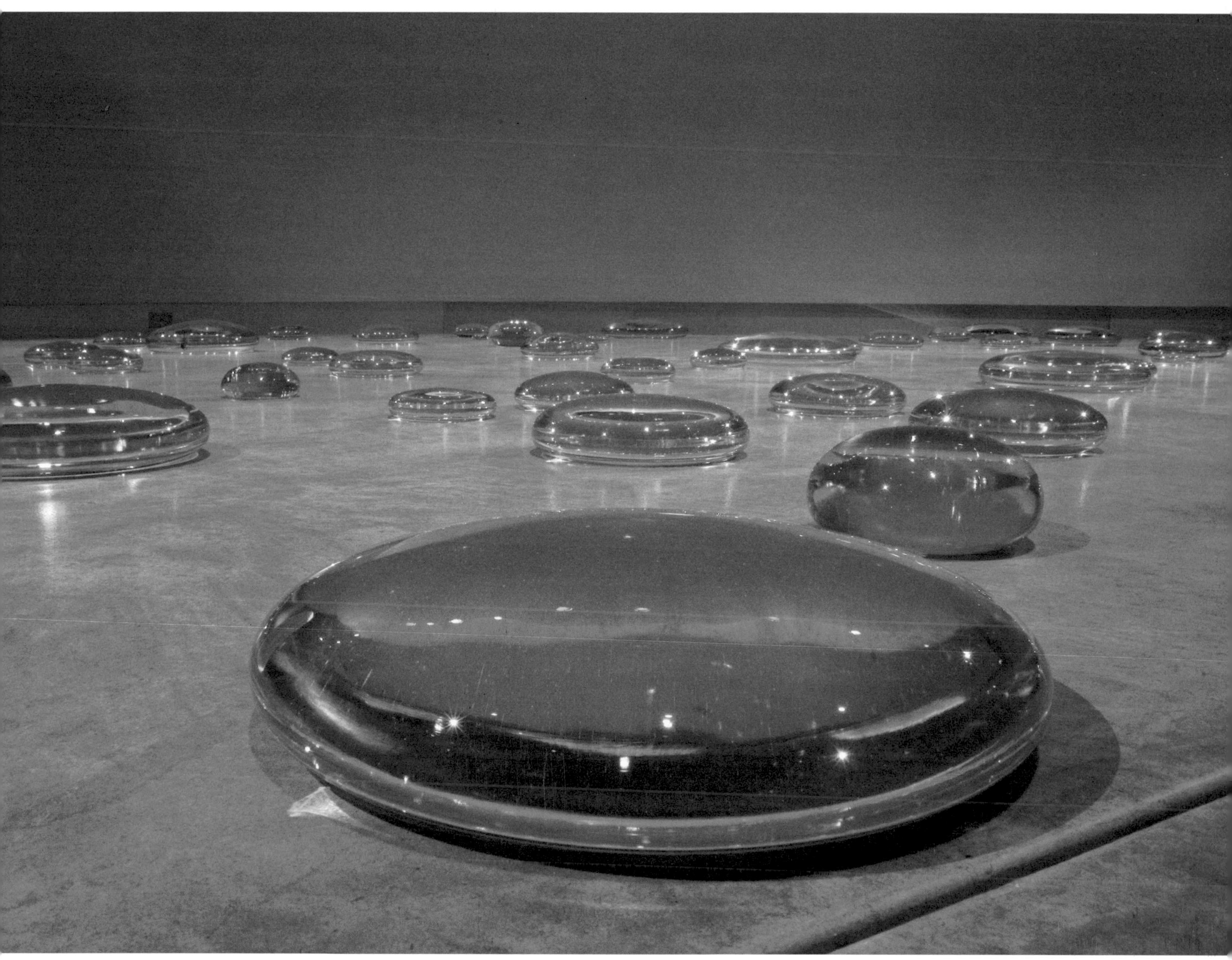

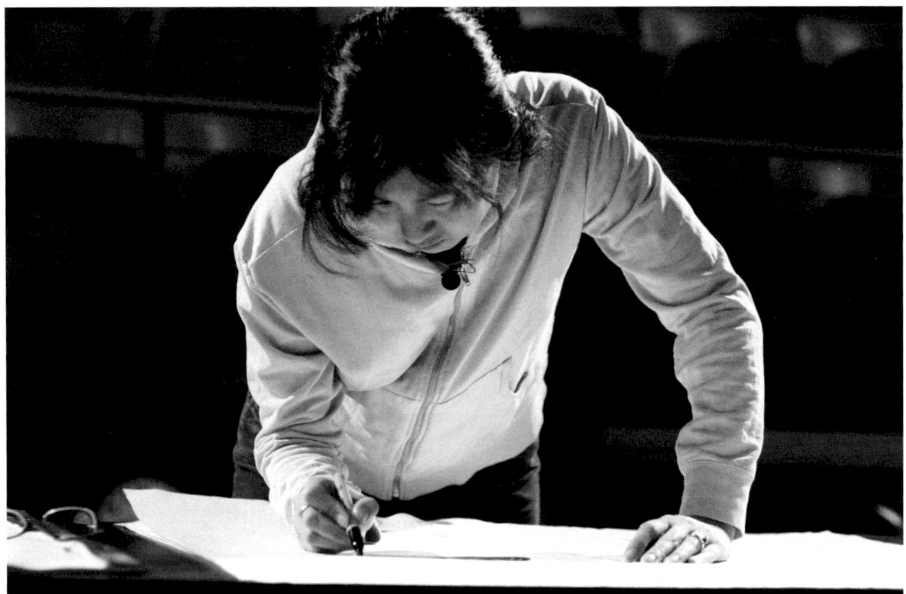

Maya Lin sketching the shape of the glass elements for the installation *Dew Point*, created in the Museum of Glass Hot Shop. Photo courtesy of Museum of Glass.

Right: A clear glass form for *Dew Point* takes shape in the glory hole where temperatures range from 2,100–2,300 degrees Fahrenheit. The reheating process keeps the glass malleable until the final desired shape is obtained. Photo courtesy of Museum of Glass.

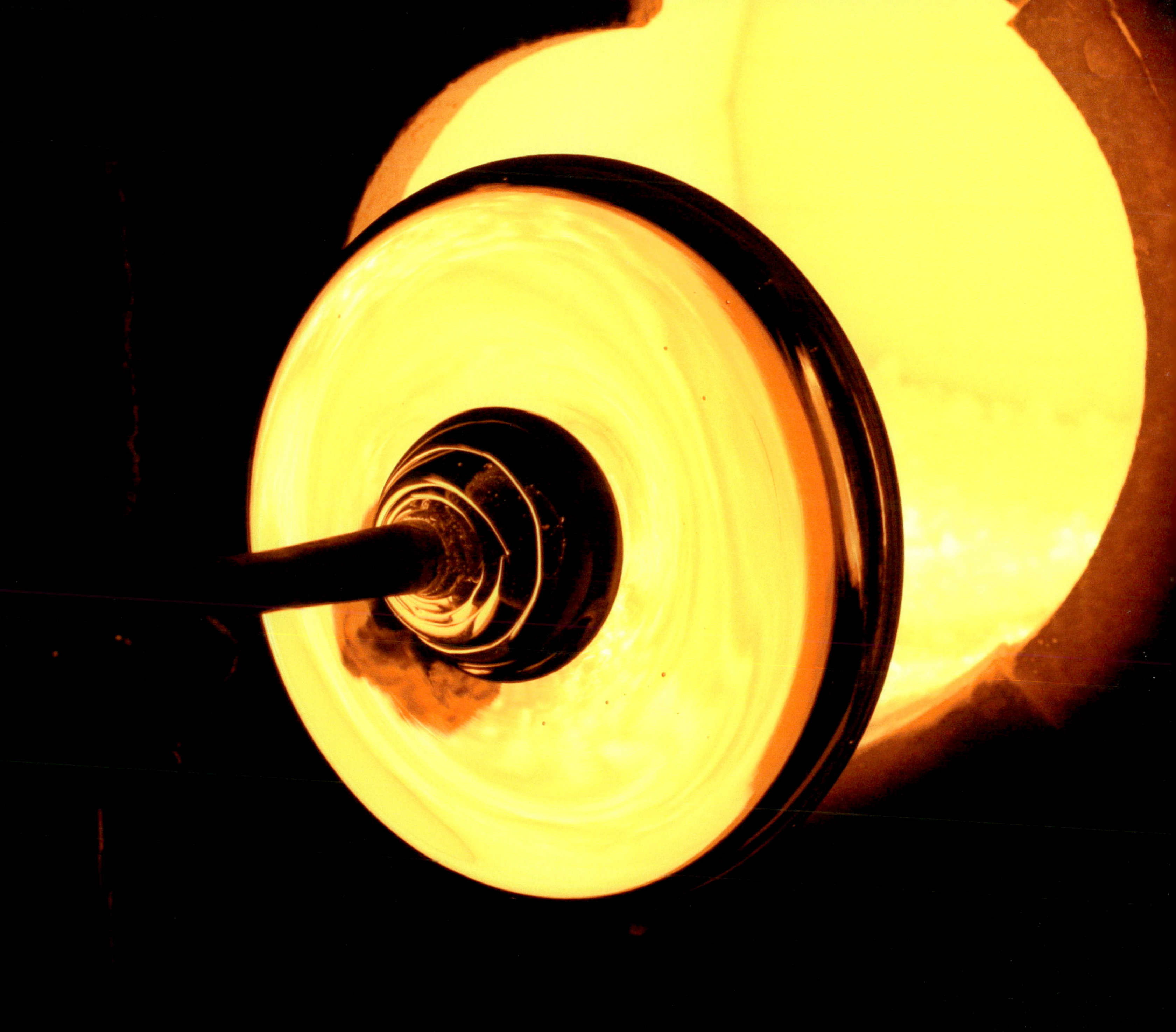

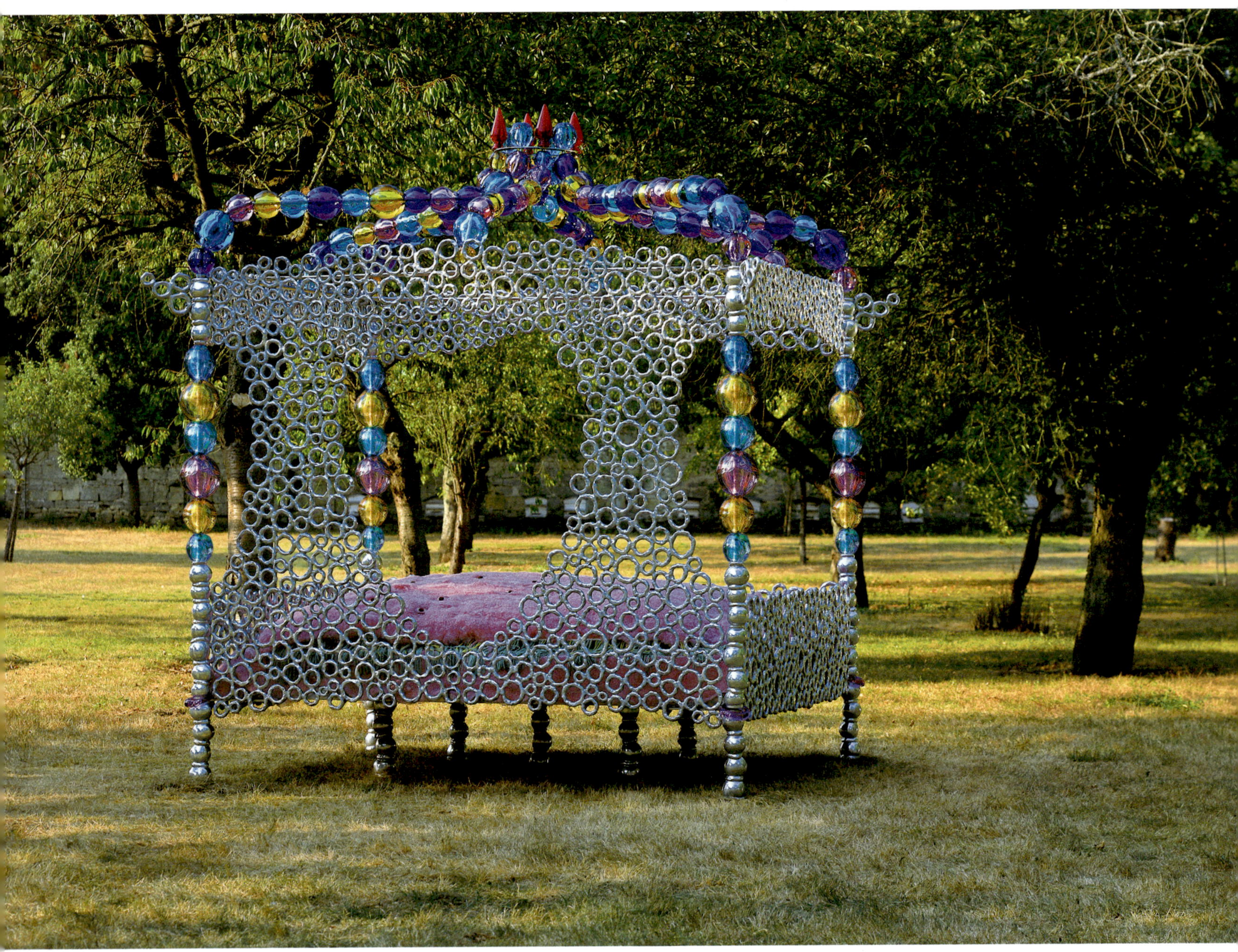

Mon Lit (My Bed), 2003

Jean-Michel Othoniel

"The hand of the glassmaker is full of tenderness, the trace of his gentle stroke remains in the glass. That's part of the alchemical nature of this project: transmutation of matter, liquid to solid, light into colors. The pieces have been touched, blown, caressed, polished, embroidered—the fabric of intimacy…"

Jean-Michel Othoniel's dazzling productions are suffused with eroticism and sensuality. Whether offering us the experience of his intricate miniature puppet sets of flameworked glass, grand installations of blown-glass necklaces cascading from trees, or sumptuous glass beds and thrones fit for fairy-tale royalty, his work proves to be at once extravagant and intimate. Othoniel's penchant for the theatrical is evident throughout his luxuriously staged environments, which may be swathed in embroidered silk veils and resplendent with glass tinted in an Orientalist's palette of violets, reds, fuschias, and roses, enlivened by inflections of creamy whites and supple flesh tones.

Othoniel's creations initially begin with delicate watercolors, yet his material of choice is glass, for its mystical and alchemical allusions have captivated him since he became entranced with obsidian in the early 1990s. Throughout his production he draws visual inspiration from gardens, labyrinths, dreams, and a heightened sensitivity to the body, and in doing so evokes the surreal setting of a sleepwalker, poetic narratives of love and passion, and memories of seductive pleasures. Works such as *Mon Lit* (My Bed) of 2003, whose dreamlike pink quilt was meticulously created, according to the artist, to resemble snow or cotton candy, reach an apogee of desire, while the smoldering *Black Hearts, Red Tears* (2007), whose glass elements were blown during Othoniel's residency at the Museum of Glass, glows with the ardor of a great novel.

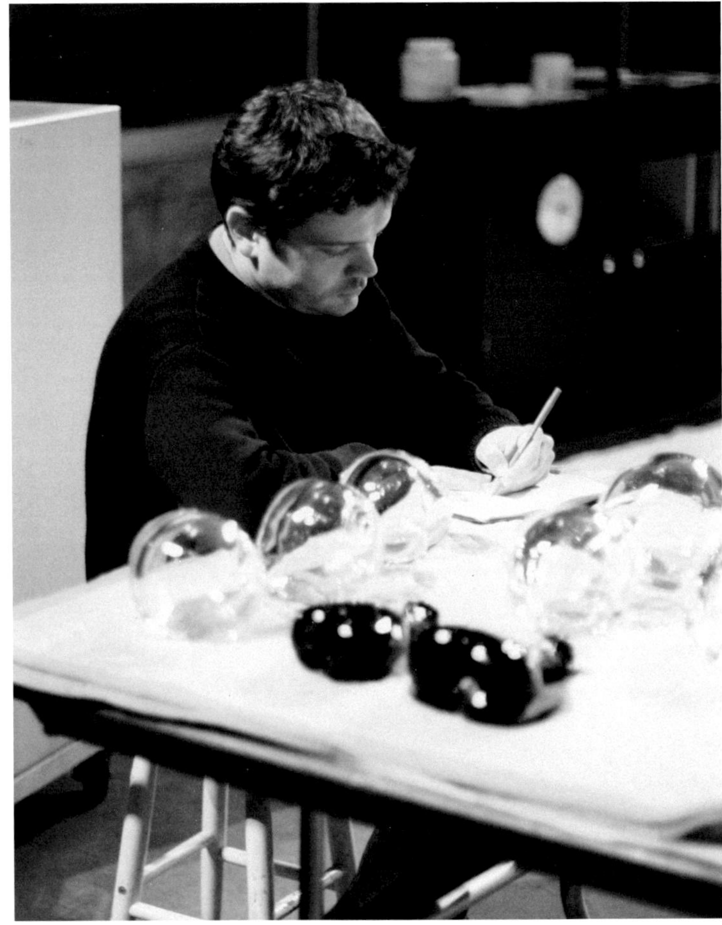

Jean-Michel Othoniel drawing a sketch that was used by the Museum of Glass Hot Shop team to fabricate the elements for *Black Hearts, Red Tears*. Othoniel's Visiting Artist Residency took place at the Museum of Glass from October 18 to 22, 2006. Photo courtesy of Museum of Glass.

Right: A teardrop being formed at the glassmaking bench. Photo courtesy of Museum of Glass.

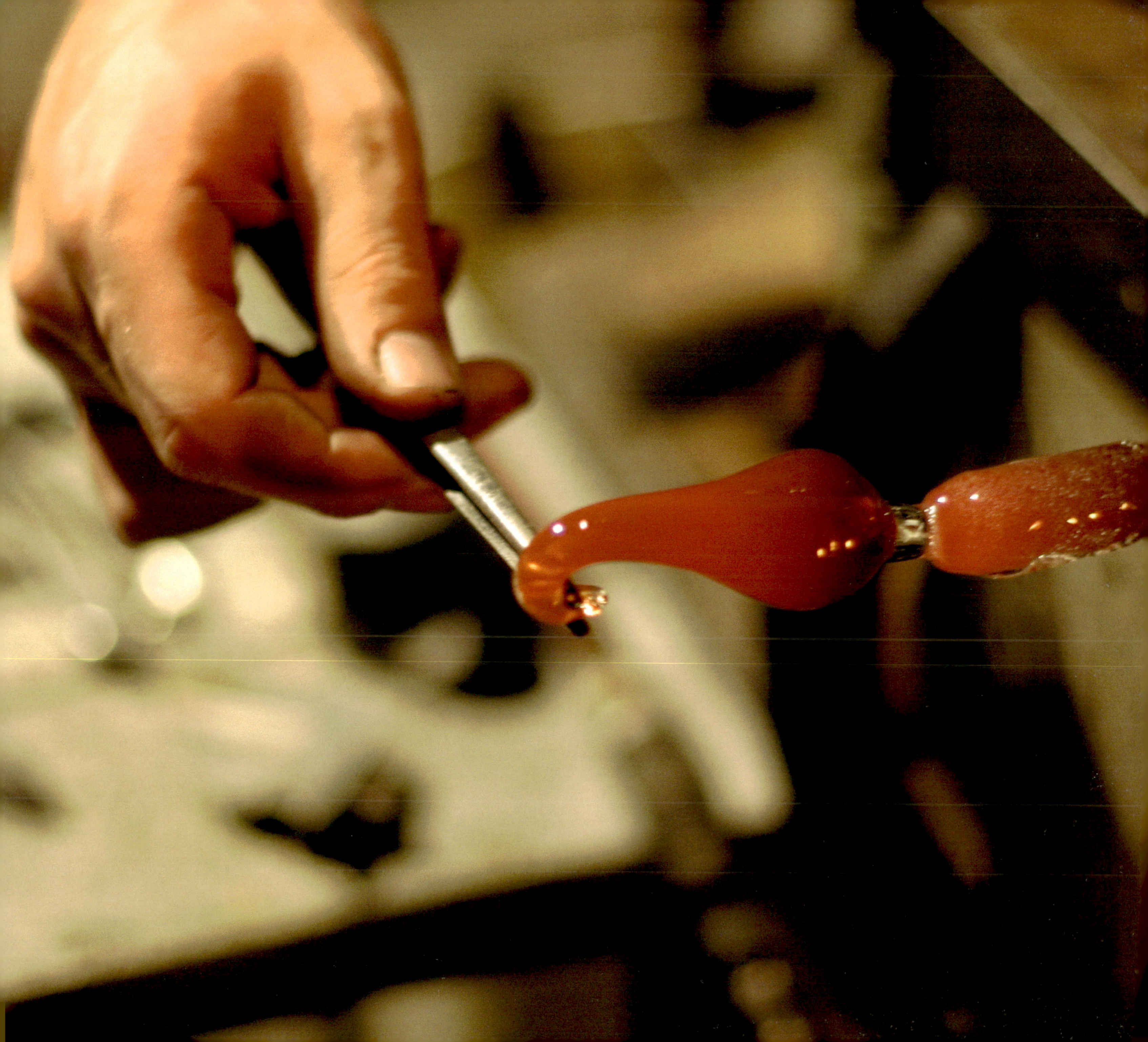

Kiki Smith

Kiki Smith's art displays an unaffected propensity for the handmade and an uncanny use of an astonishing array of materials. Whether working with humble plaster or distinguished bronze, smooth wax or graceful glass, tinted fabric or fragile paper, milky porcelain or shimmering sequins, her remarkable vision is transcendent. Her highly intuitive visual language, one derived from her personal attraction to craft, decoration, and traditional domestic practices, moves through explorations of the corpus and fluids of the body, the natural world of plant and animal life, and, more recently, art history and literature—particularly legends and fairy tales—all radiating an intense desire to come nearer to an understanding of their spiritual and mythical connotations.

Smith's affinity with animals brings us the 1999/2007 *Frogs*. Knowing her penchant for narratives with undertones of creation and sexuality, we are also reminded of Bruno Bettelheim's interpretation of the frog's significance in legends, where its transformation from aquatic tadpole to terrestrial frog can be seen as reminiscent of our own move from the moist womb to dry land, and therefore its power to symbolize our birth, sexual development, and growth from a simpler to a more complex stage of life. Alluding to the enchanted animal of fairy stories, *Frogs* aptly expresses Smith's strong sense of play while demonstrating her flair for revealing the subtle and enchanted in the everyday.

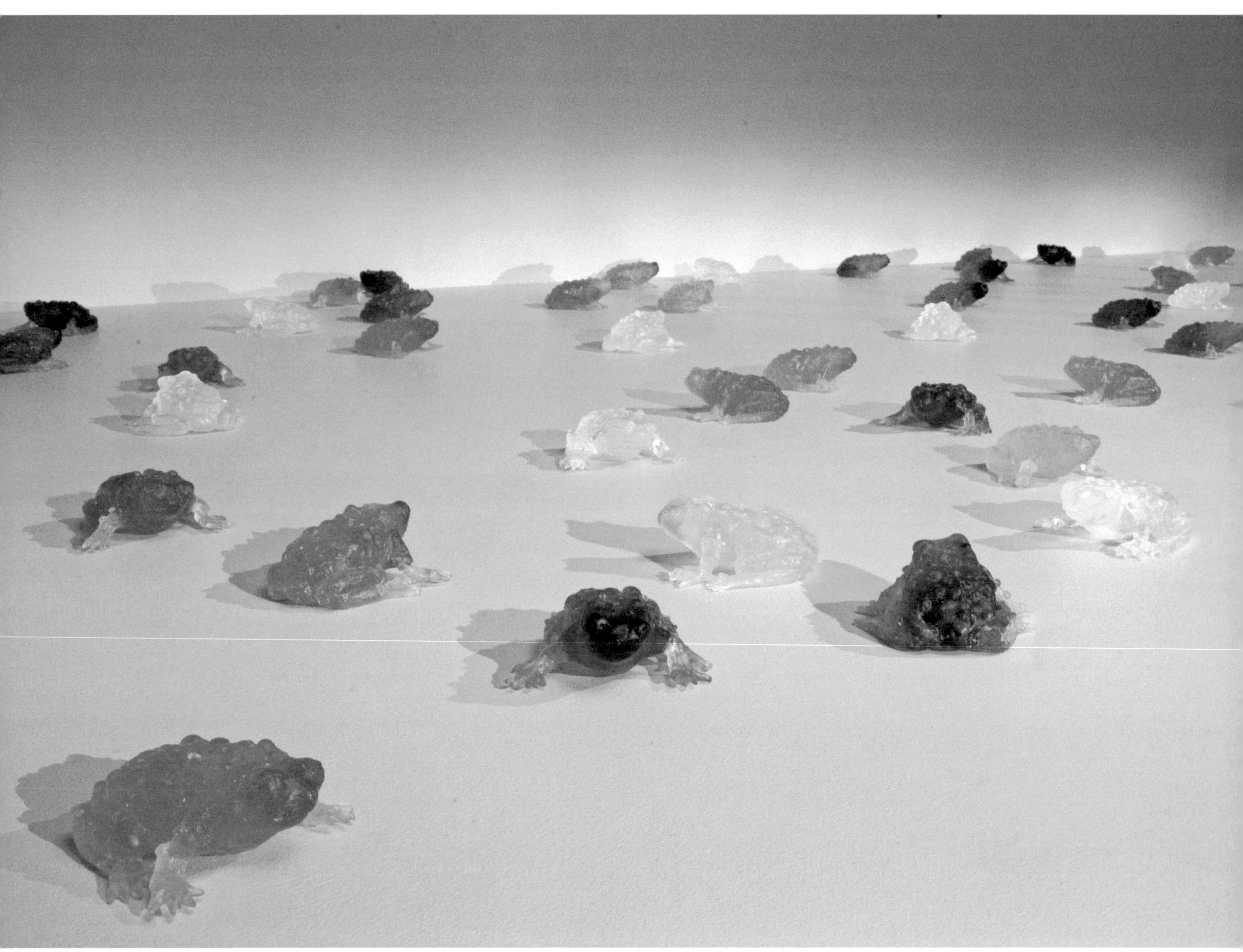

Frogs, 1999/2007

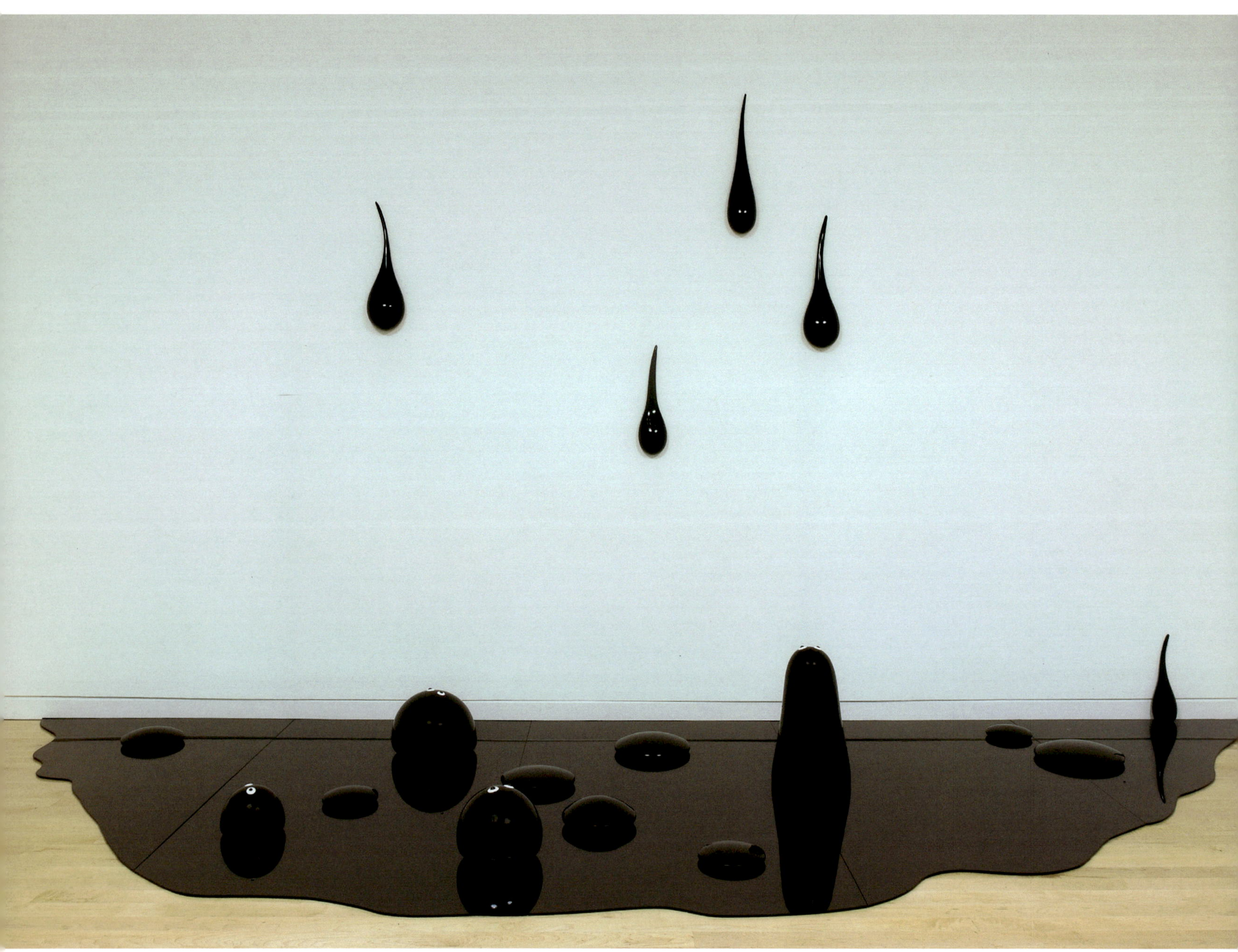

Dark Dawn, 2005

Fred Wilson

"When I watch glassblowing, it's like the creation of a planet or something. You get seduced by the material, by the process."

In the 1980s Fred Wilson was at the forefront of artistic discourse on multiculturalism and politics. Wilson, however, took his investigation of these issues one step further. Beginning with his 1992–93 landmark exhibition *Mining the Museum* at the Maryland Historical Society and throughout the 1990s, Wilson has thoughtfully appropriated curatorial methods in his installations of recontextualized cultural material to examine the way museums and other institutions have shaped social conventions and biases—particularly concerning race.

More recently, Wilson has been applying his conceptually rigorous approach to making art by having actual objects fabricated in intensely black, opaque glass. *Dark Dawn* (2005) continues the use of what he calls the drip drop form—a liquid and gooey looking sculptural shape suggestive of black tears, black tar, black oil, black ink—which Wilson developed for his installation at the 2003 Venice Biennale. As with much of Wilson's work, it zooms in on the notion of blackness and the implications particular artifacts have in our culture. The sculpture's buglike eyes protrude from the inky depths of the glass and intentionally point to related derogatory cartoon depictions of African Americans that Wilson was exposed to in his childhood.

Given Wilson's focused interest in the hidden connotations of objects and the issues of marginalized peoples, glass—with its historically subsidiary status in advanced sculpture—is a most appropriate material that allows him to deepen his important investigations of identity.

Chen Zhen

Chen Zhen's striking artistic language was informed by the unusual circumstances of his life as an adolescent during China's Cultural Revolution, a
member of the Chinese avant-garde movement of the early 1980s, a Chinese
émigré in Paris, and a patient with autoimmune hemolytic anemia, which
took his life in 2000.

Moving freely between East and West, both physically and philosophi-
cally, Zhen's work offers a visual synthesis of the diverse cultures he encoun-
tered. Often favoring unconventional sites and public involvement—either
through community collaboration or viewer interaction—Zhen created grand
and elaborate installations that retained a remarkably personal and intimate
feeling throughout. Everyday objects such as beds, cribs, and chairs, as well as
water, textiles, and dried mud can be found complexly assembled into works
that suggest unique intersections of experiences and ideologies that range
from capitalism to mysticism.

As Zhen approached the end of his life, however, his artwork paralleled
his studies to become a doctor of Chinese medicine, and he became intensely
engaged with the radically different approaches in Eastern and Western medicine. He articulates this heightened sensitivity to the ailing body in a number of works he made using wax candles, alabaster, and glass—among them,
Crystal Landscape of Inner Body of 2000. Bringing together a variety of internal
organs, each exquisitely reproduced in blown lead glass and displayed on a
surface that recalls a physician's examination table, the work is a profoundly
thoughtful meditation on the body, illness, therapy, and spirituality.

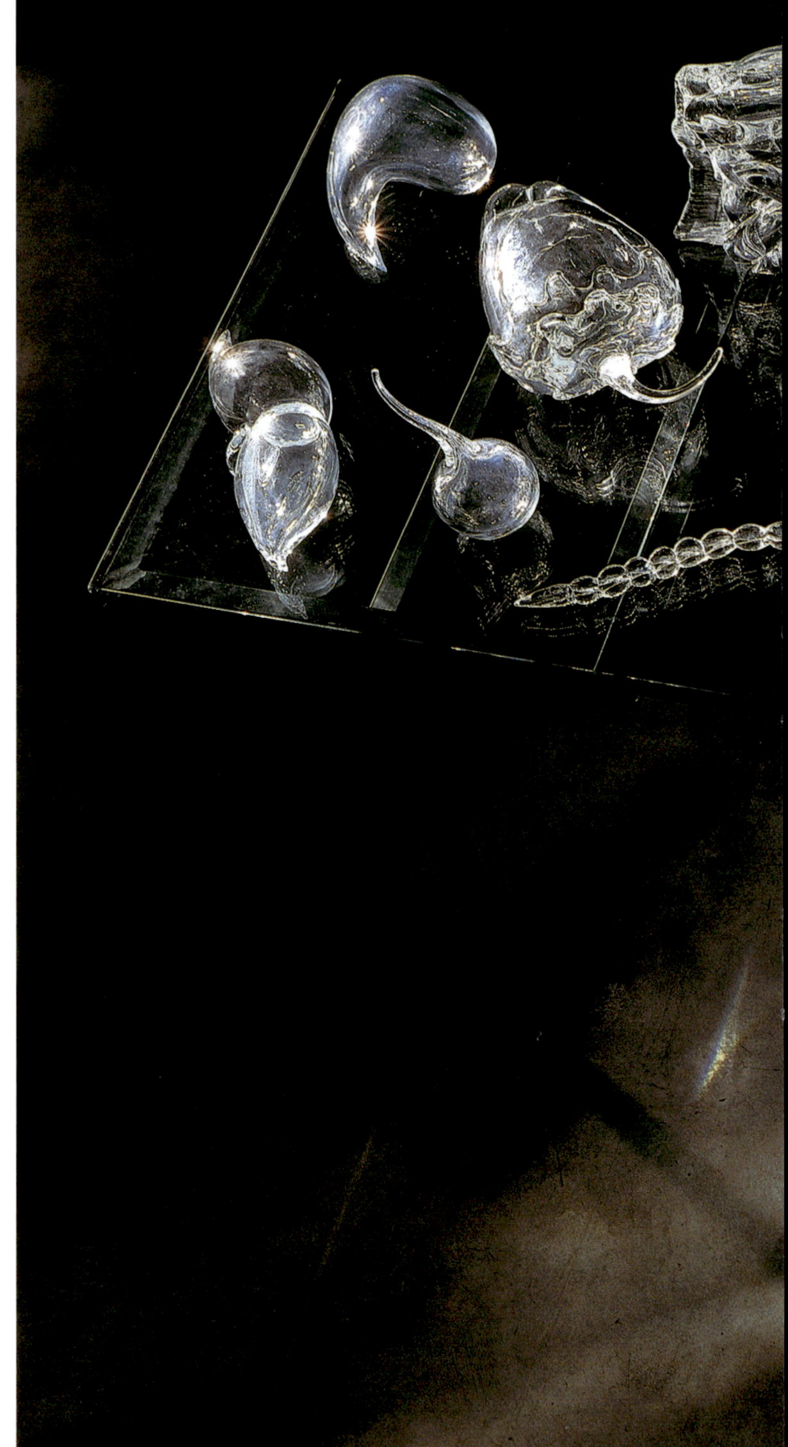

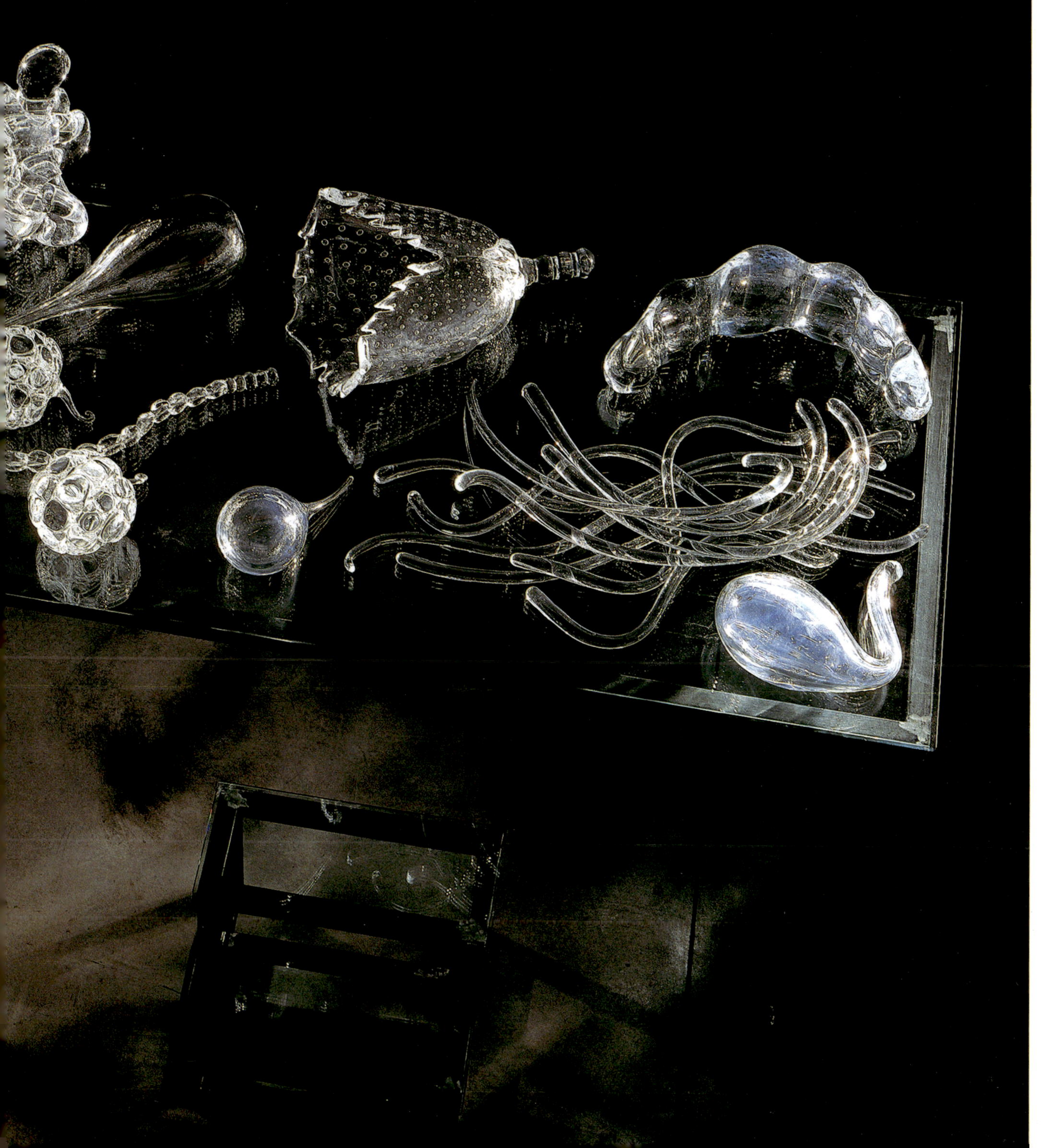

BIOGRAPHIES

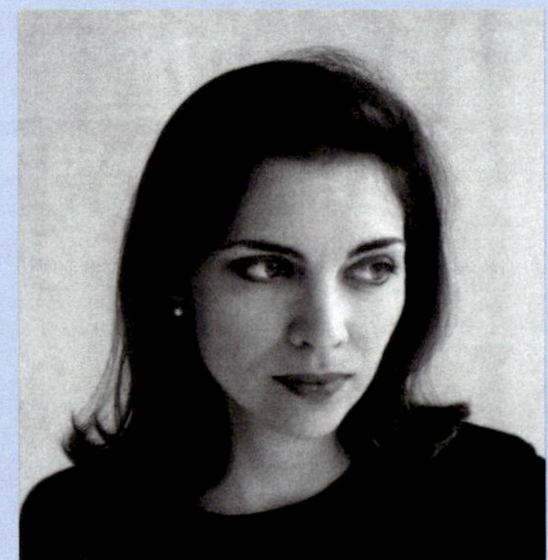

TERESITA FERNÁNDEZ received a BFA in 1990 from Florida International University in Miami and an MFA in sculpture from Virginia Commonwealth University in Richmond in 1992. Fernández has exhibited internationally in numerous institutions, including the Museum of Modern Art, New York; Whitney Museum of American Art, New York; New Museum of Contemporary Art, New York; Institute of Contemporary Art, Philadelphia; SITE Santa Fe; Castello di Rivoli, Turin; Museum of Contemporary Art, North Miami; and Miami Art Museum, among others. She has recently finished a commission for the Seattle Art Museum's Olympic Sculpture Park.

A 2005 MacArthur Foundation Fellowship and a 1999 Louis Comfort Tiffany Biennial Award are among the artist's numerous honors. Her work can be found in major private collections, as well as many public collections, among them the Museum of Contemporary Art, North Miami; Walker Art Center, Minneapolis; and the Miami Art Museum.

Teresita Fernández was born in 1968 in Miami, Florida, and lives and works in Brooklyn, New York. *Teresita Fernández photo courtesy of Lehmann Maupin Gallery, New York City*

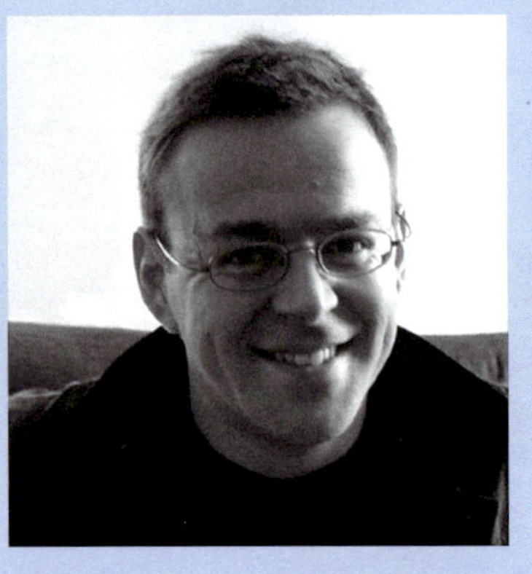

WIM DELVOYE has an extensive exhibition history that includes solo presentations of his work at such prestigious institutions as the New Museum of Contemporary Art, New York; Museum Kunst Palast, Düsseldorf; Fondation Cartier pour l'art contemporain, Paris; and Castello di Rivoli, Turin. He has participated in major international group surveys such as the Venice Biennale; DocumentaKassel; Lyon Biennial of Contemporary Art, France; and Busan and Kwangju Biennials in South Korea. His work has been presented by numerous museums, including the Museo Reina Sofia, Madrid; Magasin 3 Stockholm Konsthall; SMAK, Ghent; Kunstmuseum Bonn, Germany; Whitechapel Art Gallery, London; Casino Luxembourg, Luxemburg; Fondaçion Mirò, Barcelona; Victoria and Albert Museum, London; Kunsthalle Wien, Vienna; and CCAC Wattis Institute for Contemporary Arts, San Francisco.

CAPC Bordeaux; SMAK, Ghent; Centre Georges Pompidou, Paris; Museum of Contemporary Art, Antwerp; Museum Kunst Palast, Düsseldorf; and the Museum of Contemporary Art San Diego are among the many public collections where Delvoye is represented.

Wim Delvoye was born in 1965 in Wervik, Belgium, and lives and works in Ghentbrugge, Belgium, and New York City. *Wim Delvoye photo courtesy of the artist*

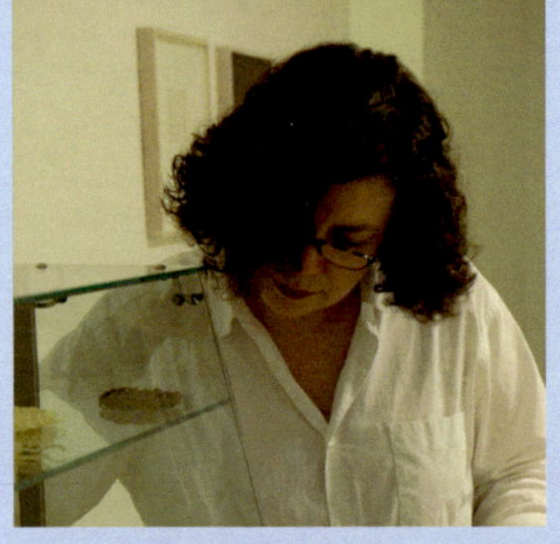

MONA HATOUM has exhibited extensively in group exhibitions, and has received solo presentations of her work at the Hamburger Kunsthalle and the Kunstmuseum Bonn, both in Germany, as well as at Magasin 3 Stockholm Konsthall. A 1997 survey of her work, organized by the Museum of Contemporary Art, Chicago, toured to the New Museum of Contemporary Art, New York; Museum of Modern Art, Oxford, England; and the Scottish National Gallery of Modern Art, Edinburgh.

Hatoum's work has been exhibited at prestigious venues such as the Centre Georges Pompidou, Paris; Castello di Rivoli, Turin; SITE Santa Fe; Massachusetts Museum of Contemporary Art, North Adams; Centro de Arte de Salamanca, Spain; and the Centro Galego de Arte Contemporanea, Spain. Her work was presented as the inaugural exhibition for the Tate Britain, London. Hatoum is represented in important private and public collections throughout the world, including the Museum of Contemporary Art, Los Angeles; Castello di Rivoli; and the Tate Britain. In 2004, she also received the prestigious Sonning Prize from the University of Copenhagen.

Mona Hatoum was born in 1952 in Beirut, Lebanon, to Palestinian parents and has lived in London since 1975, when a civil war in Lebanon prevented her return to Beirut, causing her state of exile. *Mona Hatoum photo by Ela Bialkowska, courtesy of Galleria Continua, San Gimignano–Beijing*

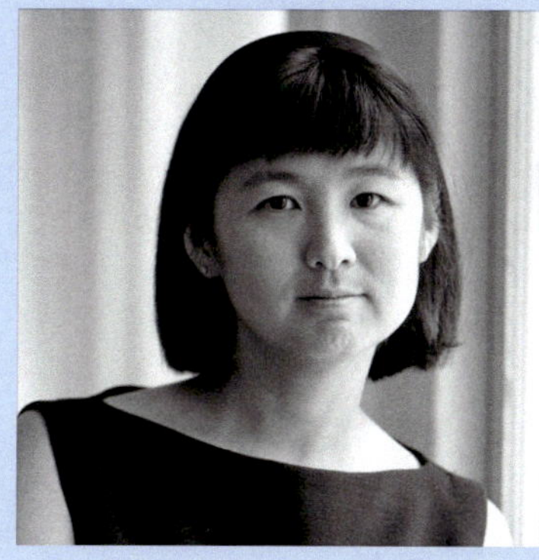

MAYA LIN earned a BA in Architecture from Yale College in 1981 and a Master of Architecture from the Yale University School of Architecture in 1986. Since her winning design for the Vietnam Veterans Memorial in Washington, DC (1982), which catapulted her into the public eye, Lin has won international acclaim for her art and architectural work, and has been the subject of an Oscar award winning documentary film, *Maya Lin: A Strong Clear Vision* (1994).

Lin is the recipient of numerous awards, including the architecture prize from the American Academy of Arts and Letters, The LVMH Foundation's Science pour l'Art Award, the Presidential Design Award, The American Institute of Architects Honor Award, the Henry Bacon Memorial Award, as well as an artist's grant from the National Endowment for the Arts. She is the recipient of Honorary Doctorates in Fine Arts from Harvard University, Yale University, Brown University, Smith College, and Williams College, and has taught and lectured at numerous institutions around the world.

Lin's recent projects include sculpture installations for, among others, the Rockefeller Foundation Headquarters in New York City; the Cleveland Public Library; and the Henry Art Gallery at the University of Washington, Seattle, where the solo exhibition, *Maya Lin: Systematic Landscapes*, was recently presented.

Maya Lin was born in 1959 in Athens, Ohio, and lives and works in New York City. *Maya Lin photo by Walter Smith*

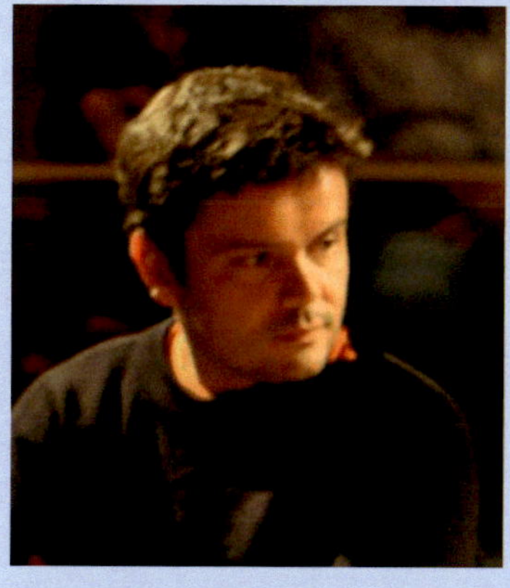

JEAN-MICHEL OTHONIEL Already in his young career, Jean-Michel Othoniel has participated in important survey exhibitions, such as *Documenta IX* in Germany in 1992 and the 2000 Kwangju Biennial in Korea. He has had solo exhibitions at many prominent venues, such as the Peggy Guggenheim Collection, Venice; Fondation Cartier pour l'art contemporain, Paris; Museum of Contemporary Art, North Miami; and PS1, New York. His work is represented in many private and public collections, including the Fondation Cartier pour l'art contemporain, Paris; Musée d'Art moderne de la Ville de Paris, Musée d'Art moderne de Saint-Étienne; Centre Georges Pompidou, Paris; Museum of Modern Art, New York; The New York Public Library; and Bibliothèque Nationale, Paris.

Othoniel is the recipient of important accolades and commissions, including the 2000 permanent installation, *Le Kiosque des Noctambules*, at the metro entrance of the Palais Royal, Musée du Louvre/Place Colette, created for the centennial celebration of the Paris Metro. Additionally, Othoniel has been invited to prestigious artist residencies at the French Academy in Rome and the Museum of Glass in Tacoma.

Jean-Michel Othoniel was born in 1964 in Saint-Etienne, France, and lives and works in Paris, France. *Jean-Michel Othoniel photo courtesy of Museum of Glass*

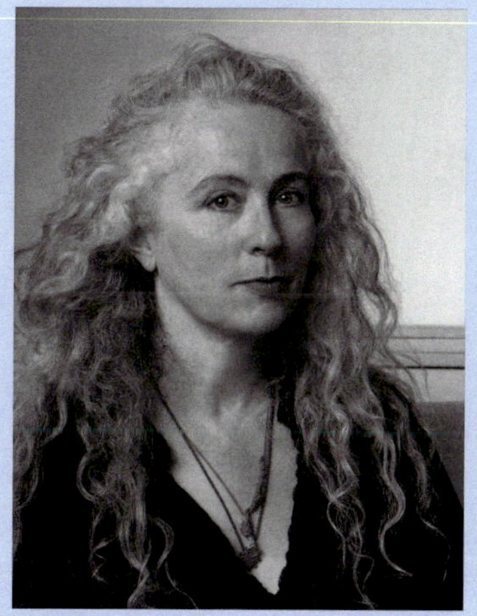

KIKI SMITH has a career that spans more than three decades. She was most recently celebrated in a traveling retrospective of her work, *Kiki Smith: A Gathering 1980–2005*, organized by the Walker Art Center in Minneapolis, which was also presented at the San Francisco Museum of Modern Art; the Contemporary Arts Museum, Houston; and the Whitney Museum of American Art, New York.

Smith is the recipient of several distinguished awards, including the Skowhegan School of Painting and Sculpture's Medal for Sculpture and the Athena Award for

Excellence in Printmaking presented by the Rhode Island School of Design. In 2005, she was elected to the American Academy of Arts and Letters, New York. Her work can be seen in numerous private and public collections around the world. She has had solo exhibitions at many prominent venues, such as the Dallas Museum of Art, Texas; Louisiana Museum for Moderne Kunst, Humlebaek, Denmark; Whitechapel Art Gallery, London; Montreal Museum of Fine Arts; Modern Art Museum, Fort Worth; Hirshhorn Museum and Sculpture Garden, Smithsonian Institution, Washington, DC; Museum of Modern Art, New York; as well as the Fondazione Querini Stampalia, Venice.

Kiki Smith was born in 1954 in Nuremberg, Germany, and lives and works in New York City. *Kiki Smith photo by Ellen Labenski, courtesy PaceWildenstein, New York City*

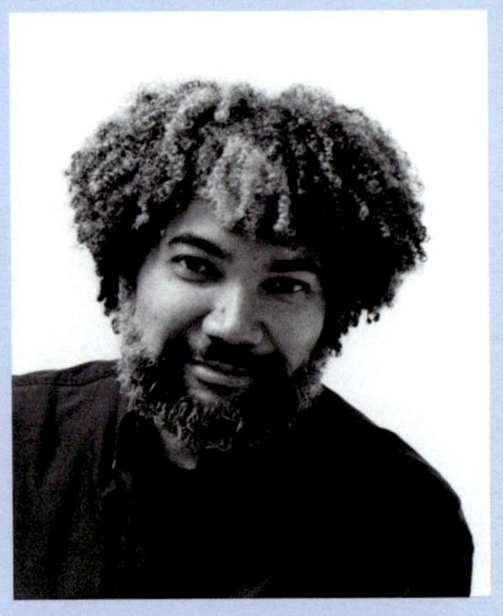

FRED WILSON received a BFA from the State University of New York, at Purchase, in 1976. Since his first solo exhibition in 1988, Wilson's work has been the subject of many individual shows, including *Fred Wilson: Black Like Me* at The Aldrich Contemporary Art Museum, Ridgefield, Connecticut, in 2005–06; *Fred Wilson: The Greeting Gallery* at the Fine Arts Museums of San Francisco in 1999; the critically acclaimed *Mining the Museum: An Installation by Fred Wilson* at The Maryland Historical Society in Baltimore, Maryland, in 1992–93; and the 2001 retrospective of his work organized by the Berkeley Art Museum, University of California, *Fred Wilson: Objects and Installations 1979–2000*, which traveled to eight national venues.

Wilson has been the recipient of numerous awards and honors, and has received a MacArthur Foundation Fellowship in 1999 and the Larry Aldrich Foundation Award in 2003. Wilson represented the United States at the 50th Venice Biennale in 2003, and his work can be found in many public collections including the Museum of Modern Art, New York; Seattle Art Museum; and the Whitney Museum of American Art, New York.

Fred Wilson was born in 1954 in the Bronx, New York, and lives and works in New York City. *Fred Wilson photo by Kerry Ryan McFate, courtesy PaceWildenstein, New York City*

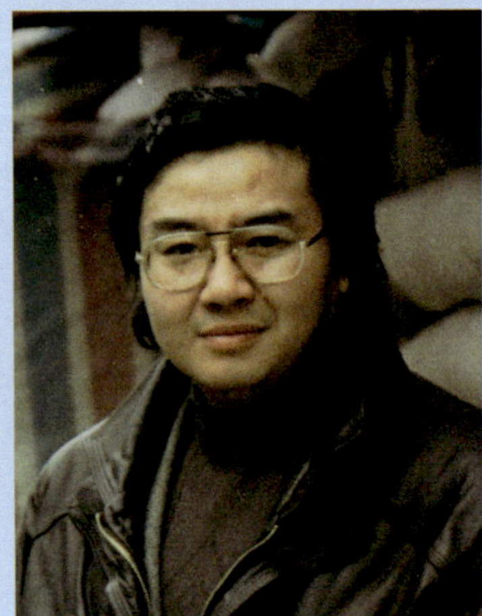

CHEN ZHEN After growing up during China's Cultural Revolution and beginning his artistic activities in Shanghai, Chen Zhen emigrated to Paris in 1986 and became a strong presence on the international art circuit until his untimely death from autoimmune hemolytic anemia in 2000. Zhen studied art at the Shanghai Fine Arts and Crafts School and stage design at the Shanghai Drama Institute, and then pursued art studies at the École nationale supérieure des beaux-arts and the Institut des hautes études en arts plastiques, both in Paris.

Zhen participated in countless solo exhibitions, in venues such as the New Museum of Contemporary Art, New York; Center for Contemporary Art, Kitakyushu, Japan; Tel Aviv Museum of Art; Helena Rubinstein Pavilion for Contemporary Art; Galleria Civica d'Arte Moderna e Contemporanea, Turin; PS1, New York; Palais de Tokyo, Paris; and the French Academy in Rome. He also participated in numerous group exhibitions, including the Valencia Biennial, the Venice Biennale, and the Carnegie International.

Zhen received awards from The Pollock-Krasner Foundation, New York; Penny McCall Foundation, New York; the Annie Wang Foundation for Art, Hong Kong; and the Kwangju Biennial Award, among many other accolades. His work is widely represented in public collections, including the Wiener Secession, Vienna; Tel Aviv Museum of Art; Galleria Civica d'Arte Moderna e Contemporanea, Turin; and the Kirishima Open-Air Museum, Kagoshima.

Chen Zhen was born in Shanghai in 1955 and died in Paris in December 2000. *Chen Zhen in the Shanghai Market, 1993. Photo courtesy of Galleria Continua, San Gimignano–Beijing*

CHECKLIST

Measurements are in inches, height precedes width precedes depth, unless noted otherwise.

1. Wim Delvoye (Belgian, born 1965 in Wervik, Belgium)
Calliope
Melpomene
Terpsichore
Clio
Erato
from Nine Muses Series, 2001–2002
Steel, radiographic slides, lead, and glass
78 ³/₄ x 31 ¹/₂ (200 x 80 cm) each
Courtesy of the artist

2. Teresita Fernández (American, born 1968 in Miami, Florida)
Eruption (*Large*), 2005
Aluminum, glass beads, wood, and vinyl
4 x 96 x 120
(10.2 x 243.8 x 304.8 cm)
Courtesy of the artist and Lehmann Maupin Gallery, New York City

3. Mona Hatoum (British, born 1952 in Beirut, Lebanon)
Web, 2006
Glass/crystal spheres and steel cables
Dimensions variable
Courtesy of the artist; Galleria Continua, San Gimignano –Beijing; and Jay Jopling / White Cube, London
Photo by Ela Bialkowska, courtesy Galleria Continua, San Gimignano–Beijing

4. Maya Lin (American, born 1959 in Athens, Ohio)
Dew Point, 2007
Hot-sculpted glass
Dimensions variable
Courtesy of the artist and Gagosian Gallery, New York City
Photo by Russell Johnson

5. Jean-Michel Othoniel (French, born 1964 in Saint-Etienne, France)
Mon Lit (*My Bed*), 2003
Steel, blown glass, fabric, and mixed media
115 x 75 x 95 (290 x 190 x 240 cm)
Courtesy of the artist and Galerie Emmanuel Perrotin, Paris

6. Jean-Michel Othoniel
Black Hearts, Red Tears, 2006–2007
Blown glass and glass beads
108 x 132 x 4 (274 x 335 x 10 cm)
Courtesy of the artist and Galerie Emmanuel Perrotin, Paris
Photo by Russell Johnson

7. Kiki Smith (American, born 1954 in Nuremberg, Germany)
Frogs, 1999 /2007
Glass
Dimensions variable; 63 units, 3 x 3 x 3 each
(7.6 x 7.6 x 7.6 cm)
© Kiki Smith; courtesy PaceWildenstein, New York City
Photo by Russell Johnson

8. Fred Wilson (American, born 1954 in Bronx, New York)
Dark Dawn, 2005
Blown and plate glass
120 x 280 x 84
(30 x 711 x 213 cm) overall
© Fred Wilson; courtesy PaceWildenstein, New York City
Photo by Ellen Labenski, courtesy of PaceWildenstein

9. Chen Zhen (Chinese, born 1955 in Shanghai; died 2000 in Paris, France)
Crystal Landscape of Inner Body, 2000
Glass and iron
75 x 28 x 38 (190 x 70 x 95 cm)
Courtesy of Heather and Tony Podesta Collection, Falls Church, Virginia
Photo by Ela Bialkowska, courtesy Galleria Continua, San Gimignano–Beijing

This book is published in conjunction
with the exhibition *Mining Glass* presented at
the Museum of Glass in Tacoma, Washington
from June 16, 2007 to February 3, 2008.

© 2007 Museum of Glass
Printed in Canada by Hemlock Printers

Design by Michelle Dunn Marsh with John Spitzer
Editorial review by Sigrid Asmus

Library of Congress Cataloging-in-Publication Data

Bailer, Juli Cho.
Mining Glass / Juli Cho Bailer.
36 p. cm.
Catalog of an exhibition at the Museum of Glass, Tacoma, WA, June 16,
2007–Feb. 3, 2008.
ISBN 978-0-9726649-3-6
1. Glass art—History—21st century—Exhibitions. 2. Art, Modern—21st
century—Exhibitions. I. Title.
NK5110.5.B35 2007
748.09'0511074797788 – dc22

                    2007017807

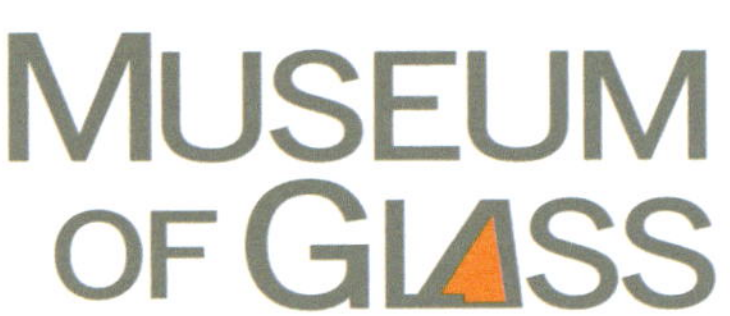

PUBLISHED BY
Museum of Glass
1801 Dock Street, Tacoma, WA 98402
United States of America
www.museumofglass.org

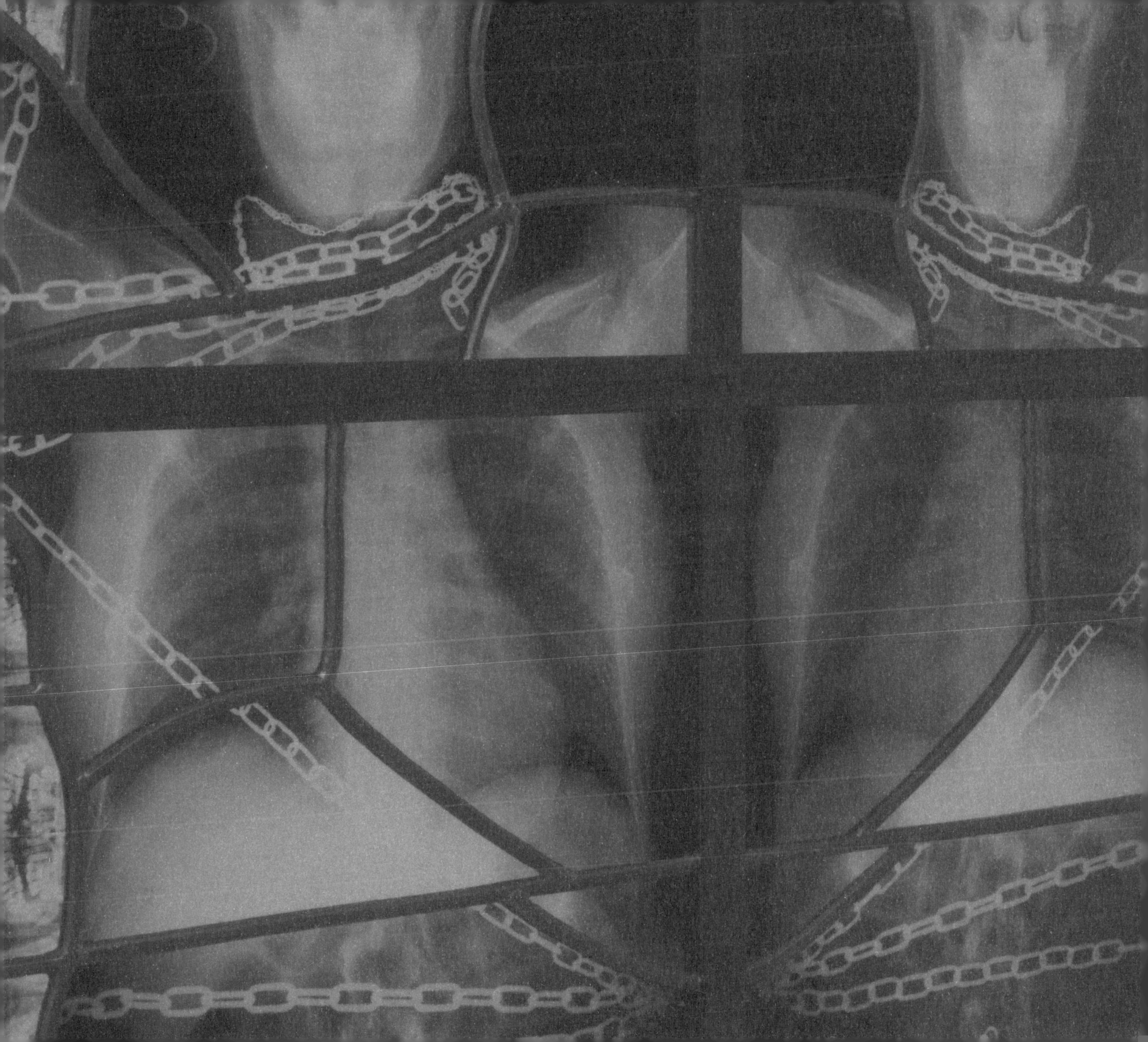

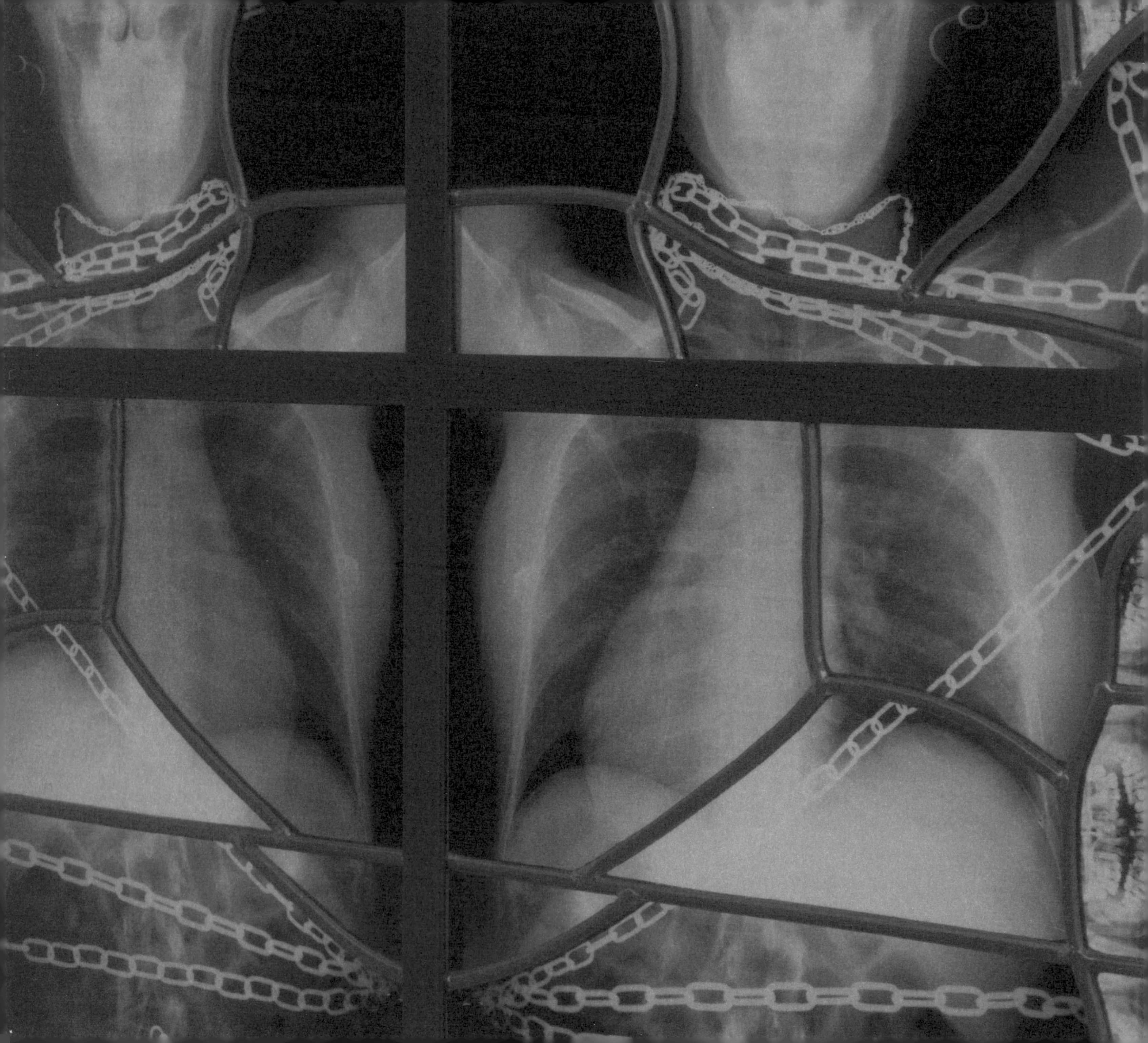